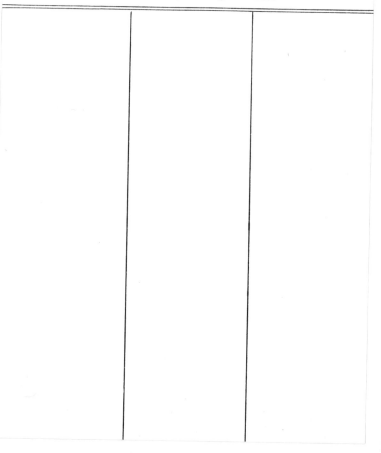

THE
LONDON
METAL EXCHANGE

a commodity market

ROBERT GIBSON-JARVIE
B.A.(Cantab.), F.I.Arb.

Published by Woodhead-Faulkner Ltd.
in association with
Metallgesellschaft AG

Woodhead-Faulkner Ltd
7 Rose Crescent
Cambridge CB2 3LL

First published 1976

© Metallgesellschaft Aktiengesellschaft/Robert Gibson-Jarvie 1976

ISBN 0 85941 042 0

Printed in Great Britain by
Lowe & Brydone Printers Limited, Thetford, Norfolk

Foreword

by Friedrich von Dallwitz
Director-General, Metallgesellschaft AG

When Metallgesellschaft first applied several years ago for Ring membership on the London Metal Exchange, there were quite a number of good reasons to do so. Certainly the wish to expand still more into international business was one of the motives but this step was even more due to the realisation that, being an important producer of non-ferrous metals and trading more than a million tons of metals a year, one should become actively engaged in dealing directly on the most important commodity exchange in the world rather than being represented through others.

Our British subsidiary, Metallgesellschaft Limited, has now been dealing on the Metal Exchange for almost six years. We are pleased to say that we never regretted our move on to the Metal Exchange and that our expectations were fully met. We are well established now amongst the Ring-dealing community of about thirty companies in this institution which has grown far beyond national importance and creates the meeting place for buyers and sellers from all corners of the world establishing a world market price, representing their interests and reflecting the situation not only in a special world market but trends in the world economy. When the rather exclusive London Metal Exchange opened its doors to a

Frankfurt company they were not really letting a "newcomer" into the City. Through its founder family, the Mertons, Metall-gesellschaft itself has British roots. Before World War I, Metall-gesellschaft was represented through its sister company, Henry R. Merton & Co. Ltd. on the Metal Exchange. Like the Metal Exchange, Metallgesellschaft are approaching their centenary year and, therefore, Metallgesellschaft have more than one good reason to sponsor this book.

Recently problems in the commodity sphere have developed into a political topic and there has been a good deal of often unfounded criticism of commodity exchanges. The London Metal Exchange is a complicated but highly efficient instrument and once fully under-stood and employed, it provides an invaluable service to both producers and consumers, to their mutual benefit. We wish to make a contribution towards a better understanding of the basis, organisation and mechanism of the London Metal Exchange and therefore are pleased to present Robert Gibson-Jarvie's book to the public.

Contents

                                                              Page

Foreword   iii
by Friedrich von Dallwitz
Director-General, Metallgesellschaft AG

Introduction   1
by Wallace Jackson
Commodities Editor, The Times

Part One

1. A Brief Historical Outline   7
    The beginnings of the LME. The Company is established.
    The Ring. The Metal Market & Exchange Company
    comes into being.

2. The LME Today   14
    The Metal Market & Exchange Company. The
    Committee of Subscribers. Board and Committee jointly.
    The Rules and Regulations. Membership.
    The collective security of the Exchange. Summing up.

Part Two *Page*

3. The Contracts and the Metals 29

4. The Copper Contracts 34
The Secretan Syndicate. The contract is modified.
Further attempts at control – the Amalgamated Copper
Company. Copper – and cartels – between the world
wars. The International Copper Cartel. The three-tier
copper contract on the LME. CIPEC and other outside
bodies. The future of the copper market on the LME.

5. Tin and the Tin Contracts 49
Early history. The early LME tin contracts. The tin
market between the world wars. The tin market since
the Second World War. Sterling devaluation. The high
grade tin contract.

6. Lead and Zinc 70
The LME and the contracts before the First World War.
Producer cartels before the First World War. The First
World War. The lead and zinc markets between the
wars. The Second World War. The markets re-opened.
The lead and zinc contracts after the Second World War.

7. The Silver Market on the LME 88
Silver once again on the LME. Dealings commence.
The sterling situation in 1969. A longer contract is
proposed. The pound sterling floated.

Part Three

8. Ring Dealing 99
The "continuous market" emerges. The coming of the
speculator. The Ring. Kerb dealings. Pre-market or
inter-office dealings. Trading in the Ring. In sum . . .

Part Four   *Page*

9. Hedging on the LME   119
    Selling or "short" hedge. Buying or "long" hedge.
    Selling hedge by a producer. Hedging by an importer or
    fabricator. Summing up.

10. Carries on the LME   127
    Rates for carries. The "half and half" carry. Carries as
    an exercise in their own right.

11. Options   132
    Trading against options. Granting options.

12. Pricing   136
    Contracts for physical material between producer and
    fabricator or importer.

13. Settlement Price   140

14. Value Added Tax, Exchange Control and Other
    Outside Influences   144

Postscript   153

Appendix 1: Glossary   157

Appendix 2: Ring Trading Times   165

Appendix 3: LME Registered Brands   166

Appendix 4: Example of LME Contract   176

Index   189

Introduction

by Wallace Jackson
Commodities Editor, The Times

All the way from crude bartering to the sophisticated terminal market, commodity trading has been the bedrock of commerce; like the poor, commodity markets have always been with us and today 50% of world trade is based upon them. One simple law, that of supply and demand, is at the root of all trading and it therefore follows that there must be a forum in which producer and consumer can meet to bargain. That forum is the commodity market.

But over the years the commodity markets have become more complex and complicated and as a result the field has increasingly been left to the expert, with sporadic forays by the economist. The layman has been far more concerned about, if not involved in, the equity markets with their so-called glamour stocks, takeovers, mergers, collapses and the like. While deals like the GEC-AEI merger have been followed with breathless interest, upheavals in one commodity market or another, for whatever cause, have passed relatively unremarked by those not intimately concerned.

However, over the last couple of years, and particularly since the commodity prices explosion of 1974, the picture has changed. Indeed, the "wind of change" began to blow as the strength and potency of the Organisation of Petroleum Exporting Countries developed from relatively humble beginnings in 1960 to the point where, in the first half of the seventies OPEC had become a cartel of oil producers capable of holding the developed world to ransom in the autumn of 1973 by both starting the escalator of rising prices and cutting back production.

1

There can be no question that the success of OPEC as a producers' cartel has fired the imagination of producers of other commodities in the developing world and now, from the upper echelons of government down to the man in the street, everyone is awake to the fact that developed and developing nations alike are deeply affected by what goes on in the world of dealing in copper, tin, coffee, cocoa, sugar and the like.

Now the air is thick with high-level discussions of agreements and pacts; the setting up of buffer stocks; the need to "stabilise" prices; the needs of the producers and the role of the consumers. At the lower, grass roots, level, the man disenchanted with the equity markets is asking how he can invest in commodities and anxiously inquiring whether, if he does so, will he lose his money.

Increasingly, the clamour of producers in the developing nations for "a better deal" is receiving attention in the developed countries and sitting at the apex of this mound of comment and argument is the United Nations Conference on Trade and Development with a somewhat grandiose scheme for overall pacts in the main commodities to set the world of wheeling and dealing to rights.

There is, however, one factor which no amount of discussion, or even legislation, can alter: that is the fundamental clash between the producer seeking the highest price he can obtain for his output and the consumer who is determined to pay no more than he must for that same product. The inclination of the producer is to say that if he cannot obtain what he regards as a reasonable price, he will cut back his production, or stockpile it, or both. He then starts to worry about how he is to live if he reduces production and where the money is to come from to maintain a stockpile. An additional worry for him is that not only must he weigh the price he gets in the market against his production costs, but he must be watchful that his product is not overwhelmed by substitutes.

The consumer from his angle sees as a "fair" price one which will permit him to finish with a profit at the end of the day and, if he cannot see this materialising he will seek alternative sources of supply or turn to substitutes. Where this is not possible, he will reduce stocks to a hand-to-mouth situation. While the producer has his difficulties, the consuming manufacturer is also under pressure in a situation in which there has yet to be a real revival in demand and with inflation by no means mastered. If he goes too far to meet the producer's price demands, not only will he see his potential profit disappear, but, as his prices rise as a direct consequence of paying more for his materials, his market will diminish.

Nevertheless, despite economic difficulties which have hit great and small alike, there is undoubtedly a softening of attitudes; a growing realisation that reasonable prices must be paid to producers if they are to be in a position to import the manufactures they need to support their economies. There is an element of self-interest, but also a realisation that what we term the developing world must be given chance to develop if all nations are not to suffer.

But this is what may be termed "upper strata" talk and does not affect a body of opinion which is convinced that the commodity markets (in general) are an amalgam of speculators and (commission-hunting) brokers who have established tight rings to safeguard their own interests and do not care whether the fluctuating prices of the commodities they are dealing in are fair to producers and/or con-sumers. According to this opinion the LME does not reflect the true supply and demand situation of the world and is not responsive to change.

This accusation is countered by supporters of the LME, who maintain that the LME, as an international terminal market, does in fact provide a service to industry on a world-wide basis and the participation by overseas members in commodity markets ensures the correctness of their prices in relation to world economic con-ditions. It is not the members of the LME, Ring-dealing or not, they state, who control the price of copper which as a matter of fact is created by the orders received and those buying and selling orders do reflect world economic and trade activity which, ultimately, are dependent on the laws of supply and demand.

But, putting on one side the cut and thrust of opposing opinions, the basic fact remains that the level of copper prices which applied through 1975, and into 1976, have been below the cost of production for the majority of producers and that is a situation which cannot continue indefinitely. So what is to be done? At the time of writing nobody seems to have the answer.

The facile solution is for them to leave the metal in the ground until times, and prices, improve. But some producers have "one-shot" economies which depend on copper to provide foreign exchange and employment, so that a policy of shutting down mines would be suicidal in that the means with which to buy the capital goods they need would diminish if not disappear and there would be alarming numbers of unemployed.

Theoretically the CIPEC nations tried cutting back production

3

by 15% but this move was called into question on the ground that the cuts were made only on theoretical levels of capacity and not on actual output levels. Be that as it may, there is a ray of hope in the situation in that it may lead the "one-shot" nations seriously to consider how they can "diversify" their economies so as to end dependence on one product.

Attempts are being made by CIPEC to establish a dialogue directly with consumers. But it is difficult to see what this will achieve in terms of prices as opposed to expressions of goodwill. Probably the greatest need for CIPEC is for that body to strengthen the degree of unity within itself. Indeed, a board member of a ring dealing member of the LME has said that lack of unity has prevented the CIPEC nations from using the LME to support prices at a higher level than have applied since 1974.

He has said that the production of Zambia, Zaire, Chile and Peru, estimated on 1974 figures at 6500 tonnes a day, could easily be sold on the LME at the cash price and, at the same time, the sellers could buy with a minimal outlay of money an equivalent or a percentage tonnage forward for delivery in three months' time. When this contract came near to maturity, they could lend the metal back to the world and pay the difference between cash and three months – the contango. This would obviate the need to tie up vast sums in stockpiling metal at the mine head and would give the producers a constant cash flow and allow them to retain their natural resources until better price levels are reached. The system would, of course, demand that genuine cutbacks were first made.

With so much controversy in the air, what better moment could there be for the emergence of a book, written by an expert, which although dealing with only one group of markets, takes apart the mechanism of that group – wheels, cogs, mainspring and all – and shows what makes it tick? This is what Robert Gibson-Jarvie has done with the London Metal Exchange.

PART ONE

1

A Brief Historical Outline

Copper and tin are generally accepted to be the oldest metals known to man. Together, they were alloyed and fashioned into some of man's first metal artefacts and so, as bronze, they gave their name to one of the earliest distinguishable stages of man's progress towards being a maker and user of tools and implements. (That the Bronze Age preceded the Iron Age is largely a matter of metallurgy and melting-points under the heat of an open hearth. The beginnings of smelting came very much later.)

Within certain limits, commerce and travel were both easier in these very early times than they are today. Commerce was a matter of barter – goods for goods – with no Customs barriers or currency complications; travel was as yet unfettered by passports and immigration controls. All that were needed were a sound ship, some raw materials or finished produce for exchanging, and a large measure of physical courage. Because of their importance both as tools and as a means of personal adornment (and only later as coin) metals were amongst the first goods to be transported and exchanged across the then known world. This world was centred on the Mediterranean Sea whose shores were dotted with a variety of states and city states whose fortunes waxed and waned as defeat or dissolution followed conquest and expansion. From its first recorded discovery in what is now Anatolia, to the development of mining in Cyprus, copper became an important feature in the early Mediterranean economies. (It is uncertain whether it gave its name to the island of Cyprus or *vice versa* – nonetheless, the symbol for copper is the mirror of Venus, or Aphrodite of Kypros.) As exploration and voyaging ventured further, and Britain was discovered and settled – at least along its southern and western seaboards – the output of tin from Cornwall became a staple factor in budding trade with the Mediterranean states. Later, lead from the hills of Somerset and (later still) of Scotland was added to this embryonic export trade: which originated with the expeditions by the Carthaginians to what are now Wales and Cornwall.

From such hesitant and localised beginnings, Britain's trade with Europe developed rapidly throughout the Middle Ages. It reached its zenith with the remarkable degree of integration in the wool trade (with the "Low Countries", or what are now the Netherlands, Belgium, parts of North-west Germany and North France): this even led so far as to produce a wealth, a style of architecture, and a whole sub-culture still discernible in the counties of East Anglia. At the same time, the tin trade flourished in the west; and in Cornwall, Devon and parts of Somerset the "Stannary" (tin) towns were established with their own charters, markets and considerable autonomy within the state as a whole.

Throughout the centuries the export of tin and lead remained a major factor in the economy of a largely self-supporting and primarily agricultural Britain. They produced income, and directly by barter or indirectly by purchase many of the near-essentials and the luxuries which graced the tables, adorned the walls and kept warm (and comparatively wholesome) the bodies of the English and Scots until the time of the Industrial Revolution which commenced in the eighteenth century.

The advent of the Industrial Revolution was to alter radically the whole economic and social structure of Great Britain. What had been almost entirely a pastoral and agricultural economy, with manufacture limited to the meeting of the country's own needs and with an export trade in certain metals and ores and agricultural produce only, was quite rapidly transformed into the beginnings of today's "mixed economy" structure: which had to be underpinned by imports of virtually all raw materials.

Support for this newly emerging import trade came from a strong (and at the time dominant) merchant marine, from the banking and financial services fast developing in the City of London, and from the outward trade in finished goods manufactured from imported raw materials. An interesting sidelight here is to note, from the names of their founders, how many of the merchant banks in the City derived their origin from *émigrés* from the European mainland. The sometimes over-easy religious and political tolerance which characterised Britain was here paying a handsome dividend.

In the field of metals, once more copper and tin were the leaders. Native supply by now was nowhere near adequate; and consequently imports of tin primarily from the countries and islands situated by the Malay Straits, and of copper primarily from Chile assumed an importance which has never since been lost.

The beginnings of the LME.

Business tended to gravitate towards the financial and shipping centres, and though for many years she shared the major role with the ports of Liverpool and Bristol, London eventually emerged as the dominant centre. This no doubt was due in the main to the financial support available in the City: the budding market in the discount of trade bills was now reaching a marked degree of sophistication and effectiveness.

For some time the metal merchants in London had been meeting in the Jerusalem Coffee House, off Cornhill, as a necessary adjunct to their regular calls on each other in their own offices. Some sort of central forum was clearly becoming essential: if only at that time for the purpose of exchanging intelligence and opinion.

(The "Jerusalem" deserves a place in history also as the birthplace of the Baltic Exchange: where ship chartering shares a floor with the Grain Market, and whose name was derived from business in grain done with the Hanseatic ports.)

After a period of meeting in the "Jerusalem", as well as of trading along with representatives of many other markets in one of the Walks of the Royal Exchange, the metal merchants decided in 1869 to establish, or at the least to earmark a rendezvous of their own. By the end of that year the merchants were meeting regularly in the newly opened Lombard Exchange and Newsroom at No. 40 Lombard Street. (It is a measure of the further specialisation and "localisation" of areas even within the confines of the City that today Lombard Street would hardly be associated with commodities, which have made their home a few yards further to the eastward in Mark Lane, Mincing Lane and Whittington Avenue.) The Lombard had been set up as a meeting place and convenience for the comparatively large numbers of brokers and merchants in the emerging commodity markets. It thus provided a roof over their heads, a locker or two wherein they might in safety leave their papers and

9

records, and the use of a copying press. However, it was not long before the success of the Lombard in this respect made it less than convenient for the metal merchants. It was overcrowded, it was (they felt) becoming populated too much by a new generation of parvenus jacks-of-all-trades and some of the merchants even reverted to meeting in the Royal Exchange, as a gesture of protest against this development.

However, it was not so much this matter of physical convenience that precipitated the next move, as the then totally un-organised way in which metal prices were established and published. By this time, the Market in London was acquiring something of an international reputation: due in the main to the thriving *entrepôt* business carried on there. It was, therefore, becoming essential that something positive be done to make it plain to all who were directly or indirectly interested, that London prices were fair, representative of the situation day by day, and in no way coloured by any one or a few particular interests.

The Company is established.

The establishment of a properly, or rather a formally constituted body under some kind of centralised control from within, and governed by rules which were applicable to all became a necessity. (Both the Baltic and the Liverpool Cotton Exchange had by now blossomed in this way, and to follow their example would be a logical and constructive move.) To this end, some of the leading concerns co-operated in setting up the London Metal Exchange Company, with its own premises in a room in Lombard Court, in the latter part of 1876. The company held its first meeting on 19 December of that year, and the first meeting of the merchants and brokers under the new aegis was at Lombard Court in January 1877. The capital of the company at the time was £1500.

For a time, progress was both rapid and smooth. Facilities for providing telegraph information were installed, and the first telephone for the use of those present was in operation in 1880: it takes a stretch of the imagination to visualise an LME before that date without the ubiquitous telephone! It is also amusing – from this distance in time – to record that the Exchange's very first Secretary was engaged at about this time at the no doubt respectable salary of £150 per annum.

Subscriptions for membership became obligatory (then, as now, for extremely modest sums) and the beginnings of the "Ring" and

"Non-Ring" classes of LME membership emerged in the form of London (trading) and Country members.

As yet no attempt had been made to regularise actual trading, or even to limit the number and grades of metals dealt in: although trade in copper and in tin had become predominant. There had been, and for a time was still to be some business done in pig iron, although this eventually dwindled: whilst trade in lead and in spelter (zinc) was too heterogeneous as to types and grades to lend itself as yet to any sort of formalisation. Trading times were also crystallised, and official dealings were confined to the periods 12.30 p.m. to 1.15 p.m., and 4.00 p.m. to 4.30 p.m., not so far removed from present-day practice, and at that time without consideration of the London Silver Market Fixing, or of the time differential between London and New York.

The Ring.

Though official trading sessions were now limited as to time (with private, member to member dealings of course going on continuously around these periods) there was as yet no actual "*Marché Ouvert*". Members continued to transact business in small groups or one with another, disposed in various parts of the Room. The inadequacy of dealing thus, both as to speed and as to the open – and therefore probably fairer – declaration of bid and offer prices was fast becoming apparent.

Those who dealt in copper and tin (the two major metals and those best suited to formal trading in standard lots and grades) very soon created a Ring such as already existed in some of the other commodity markets, where they might all trade freely by open outcry. One of their number would take a piece of chalk from his pocket, draw a large circle on the floor, and all would gather around in what fast became their own established places. The advantages of this system were clear to all; but they could only be fully made use of in a market where transactions were relatively simple and where discussion as to quality, delivery and the like was superfluous. But the basic principle had now been established, and it was only to be a matter of time before dealings in the other metals were so codified as to make Ring trading in all of them a practical possibility. A remarkably efficient and fair, if outwardly chaotic, way of doing a lot of business openly in a very little time had come into being.

After a while friction arose between the body of the subscribers and the Board of the company, who were felt to be both too autocratic

11

and too divorced from the day-to-day affairs of the market. The main cause for this discontent amongst the bulk of the members was that the board numbered only 15 out of a total at the time of over 300 subscribers. Once again, the matter of reporting prices became a source of irritation. The board had taken this function, along with the issue of a Market Report, to themselves and this was popularly felt to be too narrow a perspective from which to obtain a fair and dispassionate view. A petition was put forward, requesting the formation of a Reporting Committee, which the board refused.

However (and curiously enough, in retrospect), the final *casus belli* between the board and the body of the members was – of all things – the decision by the board in December 1880 to abolish Ring trading. The grounds for what today seems a ludicrously retrograde step were that open outcry dealings led to the manipulation of prices by those with an interest in so doing. In consequence there was no Ring trading throughout the following year, and members perforce reverted to the old practice of strolling from group to group in order to establish prices for what they had to sell or buy. With experience now of very many years of Ring trading with its inbuilt publicity and closeness of bid and offer prices it is hard to see the logic behind this curious decision to prohibit it. True, there have since then been rare and very brief periods of suspension of Ring dealings – of which more anon.

Their patience running short, the subscribers met in January 1881 and resolved that a Committee of Subscribers be formed, and that its members be elected annually from amongst their number. This was the real beginning of today's structure of the Exchange, and of its unusual hierarchy of Board and Committee: for the directors in 1881 found themselves unable to resist the opinion of the subscribers, and the Committee came officially into being after an election in March of that year. Committee elections have from that day to this been held in March, with the incoming Committee taking office in April. Happily, the two bodies work today with a large degree of harmony, and a useful precedent may have been established in the present Chairman of Committee being also a member of the Board of the Company.

The Metal Market & Exchange Company comes into being.
Today's happy relationship between the Board of the Company and the members of the Exchange was however not immediately apparent. The Room was by now felt to be inadequate either to accom-

modate the large numbers who were in daily attendance, or to maintain the image of the Exchange in the eyes of the world outside it: a problem now manifesting itself for a second time. True, a search for more commodious premises had been going on for some time, but so far without result. The commodities trade was by this time becoming established in the area round Mincing Lane, Mark Lane and Leadenhall Street and in consequence the majority of the active trading members of the Metal Exchange had their own offices in this part of the City. The desire for the Market Room to be set up in the vicinity was both logical and strongly felt. At last, one of the members (Mr Kenneth James) formed a group in order to acquire the option on a site in Whittington Avenue, adjacent to the new Leadenhall Market. (This being primarily a meat and poultry market it is not immediately apparent as to why it should have been felt especially desirable for the Metal Exchange to move into residence there.) However, move it did into a new building, finance for the leasing of which was obtained by setting up a new company – the present Metal Market & Exchange Company – with a capital of £10,000, of which a half was at once taken up. The remaining assets of the old company were absorbed into its successor.

After some delay, the Exchange was installed in its new home in September 1882, and has remained there ever since.

Subsequent history has been one of evolution without undue drama. Save for its closure during both world wars (when purchases and sales of essential raw materials were handled in bulk by the Government), the LME has since 1882 traded in Whittington Avenue without interruption to the present day. There have been developments (inevitable in a living organism that is not to atrophy), and there have been innovations.

Development and innovation will be considered in detail in the appropriate chapters: as they fit into their places in the present structure and rationale of the Exchange. That structure should now be briefly described, before moving to more detailed examination of how the Market operates and how it may be made use of by a very wide spectrum of industry.

2

The LME Today

This chapter aims to set out as concisely as possible just how the LME is organised at the present time, who are its governing bodies and who are, or are qualified to be its members. In later and more detailed chapters dealing with actual LME trading it should make the overall logic of the Market easier to see.

The Metal Market & Exchange Company.
The Company is in fact the proprietor of the Exchange, and its shareholders are the members (subscribers) of the Exchange. Thus, it is hardly a trading company in the accepted sense of the phrase, and at first sight its main function would appear simply to be that of ensuring that the Market premises and its ancillary offices are adequately maintained and staffed, and that funds subscribed by members are put to use in the prescribed way. Sole responsibility for the receipt and payment of money on the Exchange's behalf has in fact always rested with the directors.

The Company's chief sources of income are the subscriptions and Ring fees paid by members; also the proceeds of sale to members of the standard forms of contracts for use in LME dealings: both member to client, and an abbreviated form for member to member trading. Over the years, surpluses have been invested and now there is a further and useful income derived from these investments and from moneys placed on deposit. For a company standing at the centre of such an important and (in terms of volume of business) such a very large trading body as the LME, the sums actually passing to and from the MM&E Company appear almost ludicrously small. But the way the Market is set up makes anything larger superfluous; and there is little point in the Company operating on a larger scale in matters not directly relevant to its function as the proprietor of the Market.

Apart from acting in a sense as the "upper house" in a bi-cameral system the Board bears the sole responsibility for, and is concerned with the financial standing and stability of members. As a matter of routine, members submit their accounts to the Exchange's own auditors who in turn refer to the Board any aspect which may merit comment, or where it is felt that elucidation by the member concerned is desirable. The Board also has the power on its own initiative to seek financial information from any member.

The Committee of Subscribers.

There was a moment in time when the members of the Exchange were moved to set up a Committee elected from amongst their number in order to protect their rights and to assume responsibility for certain duties whch they felt were more properly within their province than that of what, at the time, was a somewhat hostile Board. This must have been a hectic moment. Today, the tradition of a Committee of Subscribers dealing with everyday matters, and a Board of Directors exercising powers of a more generalised nature is accepted; and it works very well. The Committee acts to all intents and purposes as the executive arm of the Market. Its direct responsibilities include such important matters as the standard of dealings in the Ring (and the maintenance of correct discipline and protocol), assessing the daily prices, the formulation of new contracts, the registration of brands of metal for delivery against an LME contract and the approval of the official LME warehouses.

Market discipline, as well as the supervision and the approval for authorisation of clerks who work in the Ring on behalf of members, are the major responsibilities of the Standing Committee. This is a smaller body comprising the Chairman and Vice-Chairman of the full Committee *ex officio*, supported by five other senior Committee members. They may also be called upon to act in the rare instances of more serious breaches of discipline, or in the sometimes confidential matters arising from investigation of any disagreement between members in the Ring.

The daily assessment of prices (the original cause of the creation of the Committee) is now in the hands of the Quotations Committee, which consists of Committee members assisted by others drawn from a panel of senior subscribers and authorised clerks. One Committee member and two from the panel serve as the Quotations Committee for two-week periods in rotation.

Another, and most important function of the Committee is the facility for settling disputes by way of arbitration. This service is by no means confined to matters arising out of the official LME contracts. It covers disputes emanating from any contract for the purchase and sale of metal where a clause has been included to the effect that disputes arising out of the contract shall be disposed of by way of arbitration under the Regulations of the LME. Thus a high proportion of the differences which arise from time to time in such an international, and highly technical trade are dealt with speedily and without the costs of an action in the Courts. Though the Committee only meets formally once each month, in many ways it may be regarded as being in continuous session: groups of its members coalesce, discuss matters and disperse throughout each day, whilst a cadre of small sub-committees is maintained for dealing with subjects requiring preparatory work before consideration by a full meeting. This sort of fluidity is essential in a market as lively and as subtle as the LME.

The Executive Secretary to the Committee has the general responsibility for keeping himself abreast and, wherever possible, ahead of developments affecting the Exchange, as well as the more specific duties of assisting and co-ordinating the work of the Committee and its various sub-committees. To this end he works independently of, but in close liaison with, the Secretary to the Company and the other members of the staff.

Board and Committee jointly.
There are a number of matters which by tradition, usage or by Rule (as enshrined in the Rules and Regulations of the Exchange) have to be dealt with by the Board and the Committee in joint session. Of these, that of most direct concern here is the election of members with permission to deal in the Ring.

The policy and the general conduct of operations on the LME are governed by codified rules, which must themselves have the sanction of the Board before becoming effective. It is here, as well as in the matter of membership, that the Board performs but two of those particular functions mentioned earlier. In this sense, they could be likened with some accuracy to a Senate, or Upper House by whatever name, in any democratic governmental system. It is popularly supposed (or taken for granted) and to some extent traditionally true, that of the two bodies the Committee are the habitual innovators: with the Board acting as a necessary safeguard in order to ensure as far as possible that innovation is not carried beyond the point of prudence. And the very hazy location of that point in so many cases does indeed make a built-in mechanism for having second thoughts extremely useful. Whilst this generalisation as to the origin of new ideas may on balance have some truth in it, it should not be taken too literally: those with a more detached perspective are often in a better position to see – and to foresee – a problem and to suggest a way over or round it. To this extent they may well have the advantage over those with a direct and daily absorption in Market affairs. In the event, and with remarkably little friction, the two bodies contrive very effectively to oversee the general conduct of the Exchange in its broadest context as well as in detail.

The Committee is elected in March each year with the new Committee assuming office in the following month. Candidates for election must be proposed and seconded by two subscribers, and must themselves be either subscribers or authorised clerks in order to be eligible for nomination. It is undoubtedly a healthy sign of the general interest in these elections that oversubscription by aspirants for election to the Committee is the general rule. In consequence, election by ballot from amongst the candidates is almost invariably necessary. Subscribers have one vote each, save the senior subscriber of each Ring member company who receives an additional vote: this in view of the more direct interest in the affairs of the Committee in cases of members who trade in the Ring.

The Board are also elected by the subscribers (who are, as has been noted, the shareholders in the Company), and of its nine members three retire each year in rotation and may offer themselves for re-election. In the usual course of events, changes amongst Board members are infrequent, and occur for the most part as the consequence of an individual's own retirement. (There has, however, been a recorded instance in the years preceding the last war, when a new member was elected to the Board on a wider vote of subscribers after something of a campaign on his part.) Eligibility for election as a director requires the holding of five qualifying shares in the Company. In recent years, a policy appears to be emerging whereby replacements for vacancies on the Board are sought from amongst a rather wider spectrum than simply from amongst those intimately connected

17

with the Market. To the extent that this introduces a new element, having perhaps a wider perspective, such a policy would seem to be a happy one. It minimises any risk of direct confrontation between Board and Committee on specific matters of Market procedure – which would naturally be the primary concern of the Committee – or on broader issues, which would come more within the Board's own purview.

In passing, it is worth pointing out that the members of both the Board and the Committee traditionally carry out their duties in these capacities on a voluntary basis. They bear the responsibilities of office in addition to whatever they may be called upon to do as directors, partners or executives in their own organisations. The permanent staff of the LME are not themselves attached to any member, and are the employees of the Company.

The Metal Exchange remains *au fond* a market place where those with a common interest meet and trade with each other as principals in accordance with certain rules of conduct and abiding by accepted standards for membership. It follows that under such an arrangement there is little need for a large headquarters staff: there being, for example, no central clearing house, nor any recording of contracts done between members or between members and their clients. (It is perhaps a matter for regret that this system rules out the possibility of a more comprehensive statistical service than that now obtaining: official turnover figures for instance record only deals done in the Ring during official market hours, and so omit the very large pre-market turnover done each day.)

The LME's rather unique management arrangement comes about therefore by its constitution as a forum where traders gather to deal as independent individuals – abiding voluntarily by an established code of Rules. These have been evolved over many years by members not only for their own direct benefit but, *ipso facto*, for the benefit of all who make use of the Exchange in their own businesses.

The Rules and Regulations.

It is now worth taking a brief look at the modest-looking pale blue book in which are enshrined the Laws of the Exchange. Many of these Rules will be discussed in a little more detail in their proper context in course of a more detailed consideration of how the Market works, and of the metals traded there, but the broad principle of the Rules and their development from their somewhat hesitant beginnings may be considered here.

18

Consent to abide by the Rules of the LME (which, as they themselves spell out, is implicit on payment by a new subscriber of his entrance fee and first subscription) is the sole tie binding together a membership all of whom, as we have seen, do their business in the Market as principals in their own right. At first, the only matters actually laid down were those concerning qualifications for membership: along with some pretty stringent provisions concerning default. With the standardisation of the contracts and the grades of metals traded against them, the growth of an established arbitration procedure to be followed in the event of disputes, and later the emergence of the Representative Subscriber of the limited company, the Rules inevitably became more comprehensive.

Today, therefore, the contracts and the requirements for the registration of brands as good delivery, as well as lists of those brands, of assayers and approved warehouses, are all spelt out in one or other section of the Rules: along with the rather esoteric provisions concerning membership, and the "balance of power" between the Committee and Board.

Initiation of any proposed addition or deletion, or amendment may come from any source – some indeed are unavoidable in the natural course of introducing new contracts or procedures – but the final sanction of any such change in the Rules has to come from the Board. In their capacity as the Executive of the Exchange, the Committee would invariably be concerned with the formulation of any new rule or of any amendment to an existing one: which they would agree amongst themselves and then refer to the Board for the final seal of approval.

In the event of there ever arising any complete deadlock between Board and Committee on a subject of importance to the Market as a whole, the "ultimate remedy" would be a Meeting of Subscribers – the procedure for which has been thoughtfully laid down in the Rules themselves. The issue would be decided either on a show of hands of those present (and the quorum for such a meeting – 10 – seems rather modest) or on a poll, if this is demanded by at least three of those actually present. There seems to be no concrete evidence of this somewhat drastic procedure ever having been resorted to since the original setting-up of the Committee.

Membership.
LME membership has always been purely a personal affair, and all members are subject to annual re-election. The qualification common

to all classes of membership is the possession of not less than two shares in the Metal Market & Exchange Company, which must be acquired within a stipulated period after election for the first time. Though the shares are inevitably fairly closely held, the Secretary of the Company is invariably in a position to advise an aspiring member whence he may obtain them. The actual classes are: membership as an Individual Subscriber, or as the Representative Subscriber for a firm or a company. Either category may also be granted the privilege (not the "right", be it noted) of dealing in the Ring: subject to the applicant or the organisation he represents meeting certain exacting financial standards.

Individual subscribership is not now very widely claimed or held, and though there are several such who do business on the LME none at this time actually deals in the Ring on his own account. The majority of individual subscribers are those who have either a long association with the LME themselves, or who have a particular connexion with and a status in the metals industry generally.

Representative subscribership is therefore the more important of the categories in the present context. For trading on the behalf of any firm or company to be carried on in the Ring, it is necessary for that organisation to be represented there by a duly elected subscriber with Ring privileges. Though election of subscribers as such is at present a matter for the Board's discretion, the granting to them of Ring privileges is something which rests with Board and Committee jointly. This is logical, in that it will thereafter be the Committee's responsibility to ensure the proper conduct on the Market of that subscriber and of his authorised clerks.

Companies thus represented in the Ring must first themselves satisfy certain financial demands of a pretty high order. These are necessitated by the continuance of the tradition of principal to principal dealings, with no Clearing House or other inbuilt collective guarantee of the Market. In bare outline (and these basic requirements are the subject of revision from time to time in the light of general circumstances) companies represented in the Ring must show a margin of solvency of not less than £500,000, and in addition procure an independent bank guarantee in a like sum. Where such a company is itself the subsidiary of a larger organisation, then the latter must also guarantee its subsidiary up to an amount fixed by the Board and the Committee. (There are in addition certain further requirements, but these will be studied in the paragraphs dealing with the collective security of the Market.)

Once established with a representative subscriber, a company may proceed to nominate one or more authorised clerks to trade in the Ring on its behalf. The approval for this purpose of authorised clerks is once again a matter for the Committee (or rather, the Standing Committee), and their decision will be based upon the experience, presence – for want of a better word – and general knowledge of the market possessed by the applicant. He will demonstrate these qualities by serving a period as a probationary authorised clerk. In parenthesis, it may be noted that the status of authorised clerk – which dates from the year 1883 – denotes only its holder's status in the LME. In his own house, he may be anyone from the Managing Director to a trader in the metals department.

As to the proprietorship and the capitalisation of companies represented on the LME there neither is nor can there be any limitation on national grounds. For legal and fiscal reasons, such companies are incorporated in the United Kingdom, but their shareholders may be anywhere in the world. In this context it is of more than passing interest to observe that of the present Ring dealing members, about half are owned or controlled by interests outside the UK, whilst one other is jointly British and Canadian owned. Overseas interests here include: American, Australian, Canadian, French, Dutch, German, Indian and Japanese.

There has in fact been a considerable change in the pattern of both the organisation and the control of LME Ring dealing companies in recent years. From the early days of the well-capitalised merchant trading on his own or his family's account, to the partnership or company whose principals still tended to come daily to the Market and then to the larger company which was represented at the "middle management" level, there has been a continuing alteration of emphasis. That this is not altogether to the liking of some of the older and more experienced of representative subscribers, who themselves recall the days when the principals were in daily attendance, may well be relevant: however, the trend is there and is not to be ignored. At the present time (one nearly wrote "finally", but who can foretell what new company and economic structures are in gestation?) the company represented on the LME has itself become more and more typically the specialised branch or division of a more general and very often multinational organisation embracing many different but complementary facets of the metals industry. This is a trend which is only in its early days, and when (if ever) it develops further, it might radically alter a number of things. But any such resultant changes, to

21

venture a forecast, would in all probability be confined to the field of the contracts and the metals themselves, and not necessarily in the essential structure of the Exchange.

This evolution therefore bodes nothing ill for the Market as an entity, nor for the many all over the world who make daily use of its services for pricing and hedging. It is rather a measure of the almost boundless flexibility of such a loose-knit body, that it can absorb such changes and yet turn each new element of market talent which they introduce to the general good. Not so many years ago, for instance, who might have been bold enough to foresee so many major producers of primary copper actually represented on the LME?

The collective security of the Exchange.

This is far from easy to define simply and by way of the printed word. As has been pointed out, the LME remains a market whose members trade amongst each other as principals to their contracts. There is in consequence no hard and fast collective obligation which can impose any restraint upon those members as to their trading *per se*, beyond adherence to the Rules of the Exchange. And what the Rules cannot do, under this basic rationale, is compel any disclosure of information as to the members' business, nor the registration with any central body of transactions done by them. Both of these would be necessary preconditions towards the establishment of any form of clearing house.

However, over the years the market has developed a truly remarkable ethic of propriety in its dealings: very probably as a direct consequence of there being no body such as a clearing house, to come between the parties to the contracts in their dealings with each other. Whilst as they stand the Rules of the Exchange provide for a large measure of uniformity as to actual terms of trading, nonetheless each and every member is master in his own house and is free to run his business in his own way: provided he does not stray from the basic ethic, which although largely unwritten is universally accepted. The reason for this acceptance on the part of the members is not far to seek: were but one of them to deviate then the whole delicate structure would inevitably fall, and it is in the mutual interest of all to ensure that this is precisely what does not happen.

The collective experience of many years would imply a large measure of advantage in this way of going about one's business. Set rules, even when scrupulously observed, can never cater for every eventuality. Moreover, in a business such as is conducted daily on a terminal market, any breach (probably unintentional) may already have had far-reaching consequences before it can be detected and an attempt made to correct it. By contrast, a market ethos founded on complete freedom to trade as a principal, on the basis of mutual confidence amongst those who do so every day, imposes its own code of conduct which in the event would seem to have achieved a high degree of security combined with considerable – and vital – flexibility.

In its adherence therefore to the concept of a market whose members trade as principals in their own right, and whose only collective disciplines are the observance of written rules with a limited scope and – more important – of their own unwritten, because uncodifiable conventions, the LME is placed in a position of somewhat uneasy compromise between the original "coffee house", and something more formal as to market protection. For instance, even were Ring members to accept a form of centralised clearing house in their dealings one with another their own dealings with their own clients are entirely their own affair. True, from the client's standpoint the protection of the Ring member through whom he places his business implies protection for himself also.

The obstacles in the way of instituting any sort of clearing system stem, in the main, from consideration of the adverse effects such a system would have on the flexibility of the market in its dealings in, or directly connected with physical trading. As an example, a Ring member hedging for a fabricator client might well find himself habitually trading "against the market" in the purely Ring dealing context. With a clearing house, he would find himself called for margins: possibly to the extent of taking all profitability out of this particular series of deals. And this in spite of the fact that all were perfectly back-to-back with physical dealings when his contracts with his client are taken into consideration. There are other obstacles, but this will serve as an instance of the way in which the LME has over the years developed along lines which would make the adoption of a clearing house nothing less than a complete revolution. Such a revolution could possibly result in a market appreciably less attractive to the trade than is the LME in its present guise. It would certainly produce a radically different market.

Some kind of mutual protection by Ring members for Ring members (and in consequence for their clients as well) does exist in the LME Compensation Fund. Coupled with the very stringent requirements as to the financial standing of Ring members, there is here already a respectable degree of protection from the worst effects of a failure. And history shows that failures are very rare occurrences indeed.

It is perhaps in the tantalisingly sparse statistical information at its disposal that the principals' market places itself at a disadvantage. There being no centralised machinery for the recording of all deals done between Ring members (to say nothing of deals between them and their clients), there can be no accurate assessment of the true volume of business passing through the market. Likewise, every forward transaction done by every member stands as a transaction – and therefore a potential risk – in its own right. For example, a Ring member may note with satisfaction at the end of the day that his market book is square. On the day's prices, he owes other members on open contracts roughly the same amount as they collectively owe him. However, a different pattern of prices may present itself the next day which will force him to review and possibly to alter his positions in order to maintain his equilibrium.

Furthermore, it is never completely accurate to depend on any sort of net figure which a member may consider is owed to him by the rest of the market collectively. Such a figure is valid only for so long as each other Ring member continues to meet his own commitments to his fellows. In the event of default by another, any given Ring member may find that of a sudden he has a much larger gross liability to the rest of the market than the net indebtedness on which he had been basing his calculations. In short, he must still pay what he owes but is not now to receive a (possibly high) proportion of that which is owed to him. Daily price variations also make these "owed" and "owing" totals themselves vary quite significantly as each market day passes.

Many and various schemes have been, and no doubt will continue to be, proposed as the answer to this and other problems: ranging from the most sophisticated to the most naïve. Most have some merit, but if implemented each would undoubtedly take away some small part of that freedom to act as he alone sees fit which is so precious to every individual member. Before too quickly condemning the LME for what appears to be undue liberalism, it is well to reflect on what might be the effects of even a very small measure of restriction as to the individual *modus operandi* of each of its Ring members.

However, increasing use of the LME by the trade worldwide (which is desirable), coupled with continuing inflation and the depreciation of currency (which is undesirable but, it seems, historically inevitable) combine to make the sums of money that are involved ever larger. A market dependent solely on guarantees and greater solvency margins to meet this problem must in the nature of things continue to increase these already burdensome requirements as time goes by. Will such a policy eventually price the smaller, independent broker or merchant out of the market altogether, leaving the field to be the preserve of a relatively few giants, with all that implies as to the real neutrality of LME prices? If the transition holus-bolus to a clearing house would bring a sudden change of pattern and policy, it is at least arguable that purely financial and economic forces are already bringing about a more subtle and gradual but in the end no less fundamental change.

To provide an "ideal" guarantee fund to meet the sort of variations in prices which can occur, and to deal adequately with the sheer number and volume of contracts open at any one time would require a sum of truly astronomic proportions: and one which by the nature of a terminal market operation would vary from day to day. The most nearly successful approach to an automatic solution to this problem has been the institution of the clearing house. (The International Commodities Clearing House – formerly the London Produce Clearing House – has in fact been in existence for very nearly as long as the LME. It clears contracts on almost all of the commodity markets in London save the LME, as well as having certain overseas operations.) This system with its automatic calls on members for margins when prices go against them, and its marrying-off of buyers and sellers of like quantities for similar dates is, however, far from ideally suited to LME trading.

The LME has in consequence been obliged to compromise in this matter of collective security. It has had to look to the individual financial standing of each Ring member and in addition to provide a Compensation Fund out of contributions from those Ring members. It has also constantly to review the Ring system of trading on the market in order to see where detailed – even if limited – safeguards may be built into it. This in preference to abandoning the traditional principal's dealings and thereby probably also abandoning its close connexion with industry.

Security, as far as this may ever be achieved *in toto*, is undoubtedly implicit in either approach. It is in the effects of maintaining security by either that the real dilemma lies. The coffee-house principle, coupled with very exacting requirements for election to Ring membership, has served the market well for very many years. If extraneous factors – inflation, ever larger volume due to the

25

wider use of the Exchange and the like – are to make that principle too costly, what then? The answer probably lies in some form of compromise: weighing a measure not so much of restriction *per se* as of disclosure, against the mounting costs of the established structure. Whilst the security of the LME as to its Ring members therefore is indeed strong, the means by which it has been achieved to date may well require modification in the light of present and future circumstances outside the control of the market itself.

Such modification – for no actual departure from basic and accepted principles has been envisaged – forms a very major topic in LME discussions. A rewriting of market procedure which will encompass the facility for members of the Ring to net-out their open positions within the "envelope" of the traditional LME principal-to-principal trading is now well advanced. It is at this time much too early to set down in detail what form the solution to the problem is likely to take; but it is by now reasonably certain that changes will be made in order to arrive at a workable solution.

The expansion of LME trading and pricing worldwide – or virtually so – and the very much more varied nature of the interests now taking advantage of its facilities make some movement in this direction both unavoidable and desirable.

Summing up.

Having traced the course of the LME's development up to the present time, it remains to consider the metals themselves and how the contracts in use for each have been tailored to suit both Market dealing and the use of the LME as a source of physical supply. The metals currently traded are copper, tin, lead, zinc and silver. In the ensuing section each will be treated separately, and the evolution of the several contracts outlined against the background of physical and Market trading. At the same time, we shall note the use of warehouse warrants, and the significance of the changing pattern of stocks in warehouse.

From this point, a comprehensive review of how the LME is actually used in daily trading for purposes – at one and the same time – of pricing, hedging and as a source of marginal supplies, will make very much more sense than if it had been attempted earlier. The reader's patience is therefore to be further strained before arriving at the heart of the matter. But, without a grasp of this essential background, the real subject of the picture might well appear so unfocused as to be without meaning.

PART TWO

3

The Contracts and the Metals

If dealings in the Ring are the heart of the Metal Exchange, then the standard contracts represent the essential fibres of Ring trading. The earliest and most tentative beginnings of dealing to a formalised contract date from before the establishment of the LME as an organised body. The dealers in arrivals worked out – or by chance and usage happened upon – a more or less unvarying set of conditions upon which they could base their forward transactions. In 1883 the first official contracts, sanctioned by the young Metal Exchange, made their appearance. At the time, they only covered dealings in copper and tin: these being the only metals where trading was on a scale and of a pattern which could make any crystallisation of market terms and procedures practicable or indeed worthwhile.

Originally, there were four standard contracts covering both these metals: (a) for sale of metal in warehouse for a fixed date, (b) the same, but with an open prompt date, (c) for metal "now landing" and (d) for sale "on arrival". The first of these was to become the prototype of the standard contract as it is understood today: sale of metal in warehouse at an agreed price, prompt on an agreed date.

These early contracts also made genuine attempts at polarising the acceptable quality of metal which might constitute a good delivery against them. For copper, the "chips" were Chile bars assaying not less than 96% copper, though brands assaying down to 93% were acceptable on forfeit of a discount.

At this period, the now uniform seller's choice of point of delivery under the contract was instituted. The reasons for this particular emphasis are not far to seek. Were the choice of location of the material to rest with the buyer, then every member would be compelled to hold larger than necessary stocks in order to be in a position to deliver in a warehouse of the buyer's choosing, whenever that member found himself a seller.

Other terms for eventual embodiment in the contracts were worked out, codified and so found their way into the "fine print" on the documents themselves. Such terms include weights and weight allowances, procedure to be followed in the event of dispute and – latterly – mention of the foreign exchange requirements affecting British subjects taking up warrants in an overseas warehouse. The reasoning behind these requirements was that, by such purchases of commodities overseas an outflow of sterling might ensue which ought at least to be known and therefore controllable if it should prove necessary.

The Committee emerged as the body regulating the contracts, and generally overseeing due observance of the terms by now embodied in them. An arbitration service was introduced – saving both time and litigation costs for those who opted to make use of it in the event of a dispute – and strict rules were evolved for procedure in the event of failure to deliver or take up under an LME contract, or to make due payment on the prompt date.

It should be emphasised at this point that the LME standard contracts are fully enforceable at law. They have been proven by cases in the courts to be outwith the provisions of the Gaming Acts as to the enforceability of due performance. This is because of the unconditional commitment by the seller to deliver the tonnage at the price on the prompt date. There is no *force majeure* clause in an LME contract. (There are provisions in the Rules which make allowance for performance as to delivery being temporarily frustrated by strike or other contingency.) The basis of the contracts rests on the fact that they constitute a firm sale of metal even though delivery be on a date in the future: and not merely the sale of the right to purchase on the future date specified.

Being at root a delivery market, and not one geared solely to "paper" trading, the LME has perforce to be constantly on the *qui vive* for changes in conditions in industry which might affect the usefulness or even the validity of the contracts. This continuous review of conditions as they may affect producer, merchant, broker or fabricator is arguably one of the most vital functions of the Committee – whose members are charged with responsibility for the contracts. These contracts must at all times provide for whatever is both desirable and necessary; they must not favour producer over consumer or vice versa; they must be flexible enough in their provisions to permit the widest reasonable spectrum of materials to be traded in order always to ensure an adequacy of chips on the market as well as to facilitate hedging. Yet, they must not be so catholic as to admit qualities or shapes which do not in the broad sense meet the needs of industry. They must be such as to attract a healthy but not an excessive leavening of speculation and dealings for financial purposes.

From this short catalogue of apparently irreconcilable requirements the Committee must evolve and maintain a workable contract in each metal – and keep it workable in the light of constantly changing physical conditions and technical progress in metal winning, processing and fabricating. Argument, or at any rate discussion, as to how best to achieve this is naturally both frequent and lively. Rightly so, since the LME Committee itself comprises a cross-section of interests in both ends of the metals business, as well as of brokers and merchants.

The emphasis in the LME contracts on the role of the seller probably stems from the Exchange's origin as a merchants' market. For the most part, the early members of the LME were importers who looked forward to a sale of material to a consumer, rather than to fashioning it themselves in their own establishments. This outlook fitted well at the time into the emerging national proclivity (and undoubted ability) for *entrepôt* trading. It was not really a very long step in principle, although for technical reasons not an easy one to take in practice, to proceed from selling metal in warehouse within the United Kingdom, to selling it in a warehouse beyond these shores to an overseas purchaser: on delivery terms and at a price agreed in London.

Today, the exact significance of any increase in the number of delivery points still remains a perennial topic for debate within the LME. Does such a policy if followed imply an increase in the number – and the geographical spread – of sellers' options, to the detriment possibly of the trade buyers' interests? Or does it in fact operate in the other sense and favour the buyer over the seller or merchant? Does the registration and opening of a new point of delivery automatically depress prices, as is sometimes held in producer circles; or does it stimulate demand and so actually give a fillip to prices by virtue of making more metal available to more potential consumers via the LME?

31

Here the Exchange is confronted by its basic dilemma in yet another guise: to provide an ideal hedging and pricing medium for metals almost in the abstract, and at the same time (and with the same mechanism) provide a viable and commercially attractive market in physical material. Each half of the dilemma is dependent upon the other, yet at first sight each appears utterly to exclude the other.

In a delivery market where consumers may and do purchase metal for use in their own operations, the physical requirements of the fabricators – notably their need to know in advance of taking up a warrant, what brand or grade of metal is being proffered – must be catered for as faithfully as possible. In a hedging market, however, the prime need is for sufficient chips to be in circulation as to maintain at all times a broad base for financing and pricing operations. The task of reconciling these requirements has become harder for those responsible for the LME contracts, as technological progress leads to ever higher selectivity on the part of the fabricator. The question in many cases then centres on whether to introduce a new contract for a specific grade, and trust that the producers will deliver sufficient material against it, or whether to maintain a single wider contract and rely on consumers satisfying their individual and precise needs by way of "swaps" – often on payment of a premium to the seller of the warrants. Quite apart from being merely a question of the permitted percentage of impurities in the metal, the actual composition of such an element of impurity is of itself now a matter of no small importance. Too much lead in a tin brand, for example, may make it unsuitable for plating in a food canning operation – and a grade of zinc assaying too little lead (though on paper this is "purer" zinc) may be unacceptable to a galvaniser.

A study of the history of the contracts in the five metals, and of how they have evolved over the years will help to illustrate this point: and possibly bring the problem facing the Committee in regulating and reviewing these contracts into clearer focus.

Before considering the LME standard contracts in any depth, note should be taken of those other contracts written by members in respect of deliveries of metal over very much longer periods than the three months (or seven in the case of silver) to which the standard contracts are restricted. These longer-term "White Contracts" are usually made subject to LME Rules as to brands deliverable, location of points of delivery and as to the clause providing for LME arbitration in the event of a dispute. However, they come outside the overall

Market "umbrella" in that they are not settled through the clearing between Ring members and do not come within any automatic default procedure.

The development of a contract of a duration longer than three months was inevitable, as the practice emerged of fixing prices in advance for a series of deliveries to be made over a period and according to a programme agreed beforehand. The advantage to both sides of such a facility are readily apparent: not least amongst them being the opportunity to price well ahead at a time when exchange rates or other factors make current offerings attractive.

The long-term contracts may be hedged on the LME as a pre-caution against adverse price movements, even over their extended periods of time. The hedge is either lifted and then reinstated, or the position on the market rolled forward by means of a carry.

With the increasing activity amongst LME members in the physical side of metal trading – either on their own account as producers or fabricators, or as agents for such enterprises – the employment of white contracts has assumed a new importance. It is now probably true to say that a very high proportion of the business transacted on the market on standard contracts is in respect of hedging these longer-term commitments.

4
The Copper Contracts

One of the two original LME standard contracts, that for Chile bar copper was also the first to be modified in the light of experience of physical trading. This arose as a consequence of the decline in Chilean production, which at first had accounted for most of the UK trade in that metal: to the point where in the 1880s it comprised a mere 12.5% of LME business in copper. The USA had by this time emerged as the biggest supplier. In 1882 output from the Anaconda mine began to be offered on the export market, and by 1885 American output had all but doubled: to a total of 74,000 tons. World output that year was over a quarter of a million tons (an increase of 25% in the period since 1882), with Spain and Portugal also producers of considerable quantities.

The market was not at the time capable of absorbing such a tonnage, and the LME price (for Chile bars) fell from £66 10s 0d in 1882 to £38 7s 6d in 1887. Such an appreciable and prolonged fall in prices naturally had the effect of encouraging consumers to run their own stocks down, and to purchase on a hand-to-mouth basis rather than hold in their inventories metal which was steadily declining in value. Despite these developments, it was still quite feasible for physical transactions in Anaconda and other brands to be priced and hedged on the LME against the Chile bar contract, since prices taken overall were still keeping fairly evenly in step. However, it was appreciated on the LME itself that the Chile bar contract was no longer representative, and was already well on the way to becoming solely a hedging or "paper" one. This was not a development which those in authority wished to encourage: with the needs and the traditions of a delivery market uppermost in their thoughts.

Apart from the "paper" or speculative aspect now presented by the Chile bar contract, dealings in this metal had declined to a point where it was not in a position to supply sufficient market chips even to perform the hedging function adequately. With hindsight – viewing from this point in time – the market was ripe for a squeeze.

The Secretan Syndicate.

This in fact is precisely what ensued. Pierre Secretan, Manager of the French firm Le Société des Metaux, conceived the idea of cornering the by now limited supplies of copper on the market, and so holding it to ransom until such time as it was prepared to pay his price. (This was the earliest recorded squeeze on the LME, and in terms of the economics of its time possibly the largest. Now it has been followed by others, and the temptation to try and corner a market will probably always be present in some minds in some circumstances. It is a function of any free market to frustrate or at worst strictly limit the ill-effects of any such exercise.)

Secretan also operated in tin, but the bulk of his dealings were in copper and the "Secretan Corner" is generally regarded as forming a part of the history of that market. He – or his syndicate – started buying in the autumn of 1887, and prices at once commenced rising. His own purchases were followed by those of anxious consumers, whose own low inventory stocks now began to appear inadequate if replenishment were to be at a sharply increasing cost to themselves against a rising market. By the end of 1887 Chile bars had risen from £39 10s to £85. Shares in mining houses had also advanced (and Secretan was speculating in this field too), to the extent that before long the Bourses were flooded with issues of shares at high premiums in new and dubious mining companies.

It was not long, however, before the inevitable consequences of a squeeze operation began to be felt. Producers who had till recently seen the price of their material declining in an over-supplied market, and who had in consequence begun holding back deliveries, now found that the market was rising steeply – riding on the back of the inflated price of Chile bars. They recommended offering copper on to the market in order to release their own high stocks and take advantage of the trend in so doing. At the same time (and this is particularly relevant in the case of copper) large quantities of scrap began to come forward. The copper market always has this big element of secondary material refined from scrap; and this is regarded as one of the main obstacles to any sort of real control of the copper market by the primary producers.

Secretan was compelled to buy increasing quantities in order to maintain his grip on the market. His financial needs grew at an even greater rate, since prices were now rising fast – at his own instigation. Furthermore, in order to be successful he needed to keep these prices up: when the market finally surrendered and came to him as the only seller, he must realise figures which would both repay his financiers and show him his speculative profit. (Secretan's main financial backers at the time were the Comptoir d'Escompte and Rothschilds in Paris, and Baring Brothers in London.) By the spring of 1888 the syndicate could lay hands on capital to the surprising sum of £2.5 millions, and Secretan was emboldened by this to the extent of negotiating with the major overseas producers to buy their output over the next three years at or in excess of guaranteed prices to them. These producers for their part undertook to restrict output to current levels and Secretan, secure on this front, continued to absorb the greater proportion of any copper from other sources which found its way on to the market in London.

It was a situation which by its nature could not last. Eventually, market forces inevitably prove stronger – or more enduring – than even the best-backed manipulator. The Secretan Syndicate first relinquished its grip on the tin market, and the copper "corner" finally collapsed in the spring of 1889. By the time this happened, stocks of copper in Europe had all but trebled during 1888 and the first months of 1889, and the syndicate was borrowing sums approaching £6 millions in order to finance their by now impossibly burdensome holdings (at an average LME price of £76 per ton, the Secretan holdings must have been in the region of 75,000 tons). Purchases for cash – immediate delivery – by the syndicate ceased after February 1899; and following the suicide in March that year of the Secretary of the Comptoir d'Escompte, the bank itself was saved from disaster by a support operation mounted by the Banque de France. Meanwhile, the London price of copper collapsed from £75 to £35 per ton within the first half of March: having previously touched a record £105, with attendant wide backwardation.

The syndicate's stocks had been taken over by the Banque de France and their liquidation posed a major problem: too fast and the market would be unable to absorb them without a further decline in prices, and too leisurely a programme would leave the bank virtually maintaining Secretan's erstwhile monopoly position. In fact the process took several years and in 1890 its progress had stabilised average prices at around £54 5s 0d per ton.

It is interesting to speculate on how this affair might have worked itself out had the Secretan Syndicate operated in the three months position, rather than in cash copper: lending the warrants in the market as contracts became prompt.

The contract is modified.

During the epoch of the Secretan corner the authorities of the LME had been pressed hard by subscribers to amend the copper contract with a view to broadening its base. The first change came in August 1888, when "Good Merchantable Brands" (GMB) became the standard chips. These included a variety of brands both of refined and rough copper: provided in each case that the brand had been registered with the LME Committee. The system of authorisation of individual brands by the Committee was thus inaugurated during this time of crisis. Metal had to assay not less than 93% copper, be certified by two recognised assayers and spoken for as to suitability by two British consumers. This formula is still followed, though assay must now be not less than 99.9% for cathodes, and the standard is set for both wirebars and cathodes as the specification of either the British Standards Institute (BSI) or the American Society for Testing Materials (ASTM).

There was now one standard copper contract, instead of four separate contracts (mentioned on page 29), and the forward dealing period was fixed at three months. Previously nothing had been laid down as to duration of a forward contract, although three months had been taken as a typical voyage time in "on arrival of ship" dealings. Points of delivery approved under the contract were listed as Birkenhead, Liverpool, London and Swansea.

Now, the market was no longer dependent on Chilean supplies for its stocks and for arriving at its prices. Recognition was thus tacitly given to the fact that a wider-ranging contract was not only desirable, but actually essential in order to maintain a strong hedging market: as proof as possible against squeezing. and quoting very much more representative prices. Difficulties facing purchasers confronted with a variety of shapes and grades under the sellers option clause were accepted as being the lesser evil.

But this was not to last for long. Rough copper assaying around

95% copper had been more or less the order of the day, but now new refining processes were being perfected which would give up to 99.75% in the case of best selected. This higher purity (fire-refined) material was much in demand amongst consumers, along with 99.25% tile copper. For producers and consumers of these higher grades, a contract based on 96% rough copper – and with as yet no proper system of premiums or discounts for deliveries of differing grades – was of little use save as a vehicle for hedging. Already the GMB contract was going the way of its predecessor.

In the last decade of the century, electrolytically refined copper was being produced, which assayed as high as 99.9%, and by the turn of the century electro constituted almost half the supply. This increasing production of high purity metal met the needs of the growing electrical and cable-making industries. It was becoming clear that another step towards higher purity in the LME contract was needed, and for much the same reasons (though without the added stimulus of a fully rigged cornering operation) as GMB had outplaced the original Chile bar contract. GMB was now too small a section of the market to be representative as to prices, and too wide in scope and low in purity for a really suitable delivery contract.

In consequence, and after some deliberation, the Committee authorised an additional refined copper contract in January 1898: this was to operate alongside GMB, as an alternative. GMB endured for another four years only, before refined (99% to 99.3% copper) became the Standard copper contract. However, this time a system of premiums for electro, and discounts for rough down to 94% was instituted. At the same time the delivery points were widened to include Birmingham and Newcastle upon Tyne. The standard contract remained the sole copper contract on the LME until the introduction of what was universally if disrespectfully nicknamed "the Three-Ring Circus" in 1963.

Further attempts at control – the Amalagmated Copper Company.
Reverting for a moment to the years immediately following the Secretan operation, the first serious attempt by a producing group to control prices was made in the 1890s. The approach had now been made "from the other end" so to speak, and was based on agreed curtailment of production by mining groups. However, co-operation by all such groups (notably the Americans who at the time were responsible for some 50% of world output) was no easier to ensure then than has proved the case in more recent times.

In 1899 certain significant changes in the proprietorship of Anaconda, followed by the absorption of other Montana mines, resulted in the creation of the Amalgamated Copper Company. This group was of itself large enough to obtain the co-operation (willing or not, history does not relate) of other American producers as well as of the Spanish. Shipments of Amalgamated production to Europe were reduced, and in consequence the price of standard copper in London rose from an average of £51 (or just over) to more than £73 per ton. For a time, the producers were able to buy on the market as an aid to maintaining prices at these levels, but continuing demand by consumers even at these prices led to increases in output by producers outside the group. As a result, the support operation became unduly costly, and inevitably large stocks of metal were piling up in Amalgamated's hands.

The pendulum swung abruptly (as later experience shows will always be the case when a corner or a cartel finally collapses) and heavy selling both in London and New York brought standard back to £45 per ton by early 1902. Once again, heavy stocks – this time in producers' hands – had to be liquidated without further upsetting the market, and once again the LME rose to the occasion. For a time in the first decade of this century, American speculation in mining shares as well as further attempts by Amalgamated to hold back supplies of copper resulted in much instability of prices: at one time (in 1907) standard was priced at £112 in London. Later, the collapse of business confidence in the USA brought all prices down once more, and the market lapsed into a calmer though somewhat depressed state.

Copper – and cartels – between the world wars.

At the end of the First World War, the USA was established as the dominant producer of copper: in line with her generally fortunate economic situation in the early post war years. For the most part, America's domestic production was absorbed by her own fabricators and she was not (nor has since been) a major exporter. However, at that time America largely controlled the Chilean and other Latin American mines and though their output tended in the main to go to the USA for smelting, it was then widely exported: accounting for some 66% of world exports. The emerging Congolese production was also to a large extent refined in the USA. Of the other "independent" producers, Spain was no longer a serious factor and the

39

THE LONDON METAL EXCHANGE

other African mines were not yet consolidated to anything approaching their present importance as exporters. Unfortunately for them, the American interests now found amongst their overall holdings numerous mining operations which for various reasons were less profitable than the others – the so-called "high cost" mines. Expansion of production from other sources militated against higher prices and once more the attempt was made to control output in order to support or increase world copper prices.

Copper Exporters Incorporated was formed in 1926. Apart from American and Chilean producers its members included Rio Tinto, Katanga (Congo) as well as German interests, and in all they accounted for no less than 95% of world production. This cartel professed the aim of supporting copper prices by the exclusion of speculators and merchants or middlemen and not – be it noted – by cutting back production. In its opening announcement, the cartel informed the world that among other things its intention was "to sell direct to consumers, and prices will be established in accordance with general business conditions as they develop from day to day". A uniquely one-sided attempt to resolve a many-sided problem and without recourse to the LME.

The exclusion of the LME was to be achieved firstly by the unilateral decision to reduce to a trickle sales to London merchants, and secondly by the establishment of an agency in Brussels to negotiate direct sales to European consumers. (US consumers were of course already tied – as to a great extent they still are – to the US domestic producers' price.) A further restriction was the limitation of tonnages sold to consumers outside the USA, to what amounted virtually to their day-to-day needs only; in this way sale by a consumer of any surplus on the LME was minimised if not altogether prevented.

Stocks already in circulation on the market had of course to be acquired. These acquisitions were made not only by the cartel or its agents, but also by consumers anxious as to the availability of supplies at other than a monopoly price. (True, the first year or so of operation of Copper Exporters Incorporated had coincided with relative stability of prices.) As a result of these purchases, stocks in the United Kingdom fell from 50,000 tons in 1926 to fewer than 5000 in 1928. As is often the case when stocks are so drastically reduced, what little that does remain is either the less acceptable brands (rough copper for the most part in this instance) or it is already well spoken for and so not truly free material.

The effects of the cartel's activity were both widespread and serious. The LME found its turnover dwindling away to a trickle, and consumers at the same time began to hanker after the freedom to bargain and to hedge their commitments which the market had previously afforded them. The monopoly was completely free to dictate prices as it chose (a delight which Secretan never quite achieved), and in October 1928 electro copper had risen to £75 per ton. All this was based on the withholding of supplies, on what amounted to almost daily partial *force majeure* declarations against selected consumers, and was indeed a very far cry from the pious sentiments quoted above.

But worse was to come. In 1929 (before the depression and with trade still extremely active) the cartel yielded once and for all to the dictates of commercial greed in the face of extremely strong consumer demand. Prices were pushed higher yet and electro reached £114 per ton, with standard at a discount of £17 beneath this, along with secondary material recovered from scrap. At these levels, consumers began to withdraw from the market, and even some of the American members of the cartel became restive over not being permitted to dispose of cheaper grades (notably recoveries from scrap) at more competitive prices.

In the spring of 1929 Copper Exporters Incorporated yielded a little to pressure – largely from within its own ranks – and the export price was progressively reduced. Electro prices in London fell in sympathy first to £84. The initiative was still entirely with the cartel however, and as demand fell away with the beginnings of the great depression, there was no longer any pretence of a free market in copper.

The final break-up of the cartel was brought about in part by the appearance once more in the London market of rough copper refined from scrap, which was delivered against the standard contract. This movement spread to the point where custom-smelter members of the cartel began of their own volition to deliver some of what was fast becoming an embarrassing surplus to them. As these supplies came to the market, so prices began to fall towards something more in line with world economic conditions; and after a prolonged "high" at £84 in London electro fell to £66, and the US export price was cut once more.

This time, the liquidation – or assimilation by the market – of the vast surplus of stocks which had been amassed was not quite so tidy. Admittedly, this time such a liquidation had to be carried out in the face of a world depression of unprecedented seriousness. In the USA electro fell from 14 cents per pound in 1929, to 10 cents at the end of 1930 and then to an historic "low" in 1932 of 4 to 5 cents. In London, standard fell to its historic "low" of £25 per ton.

One interesting side-effect of this particular cartel operation was the stimulus it gave to some of the independent producers. Whilst American domestic production declined as a result partly of the slump but mainly because of distortion brought about by the manipulation of prices, those of Canada and Rhodesia were progressing strongly. At the same time the cartel had demonstrated – in spectacular fashion – the essential shortcoming of any such one-sided attempt at market control: lack of flexibility. It appears historically true, if at first sight illogical, that neither an entirely producer-controlled cartel (Copper Exporters Incorporated) nor an entirely consumer or financier directed one (Secretan) has the ability to stay close enough to, nor keep up with changes in conditions in what is best described simply as the mood of the market. Inevitably it seems they lag, and they lack the breadth of perspective so essential in international marketing. It is these attributes – flexibility, speed, and breadth or catholicity of outlook – which merchants and brokers always have to offer.

There remains briefly to consider one further cartel operation, before examining the copper market in the years following the Second World War.

1932 was the blackest year of the great depression. By this time, the copper market was effectively divided into two: the USA which was virtually closed to imports by a high wall of tariffs, and the somewhat less restricted European markets. (The UK for example was then and still remains a free market as to import duties on copper from any source.) However, various political linings-up began to take shape, with Britain buying as far as possible from Empire sources, and France, Belgium and Germany all in varying degree associated with Katanga, Rhodesia and Eastern Europe. Chile and Peru were at the time marginal exporters only: though this situation was not to be a permanent one. Prices meanwhile remained low, with standard at or around £30 per ton or a little over.

In America, the very large unconsumed stocks were a continuing embarrassment. Restrictions had been placed on domestic sales from stocks, and a maximum quota also on sales from new production. Because of these restrictions, American producers had recourse only to the export market in order to divest themselves of at least some of their very heavy stocks, as well as to make over-the-quota sales of new output. Accordingly, American exports of copper rose from around 125,000 tons average to over a quarter of a million tons in 1934. Standard in London was further weakened to £25 12s 6d. It was clear that US selling, combined with increasing output from the "new" producers and the virtual collapse at the time of the important German market were between them forcing copper prices to completely uneconomic levels. As an attempt to regularise trade in some way, the International Copper Cartel was set up in 1935.

The International Copper Cartel.

Members of the new cartel agreed to restrict output to 75% of capacity from June of the year of its institution, and American exports were likewise to be pegged at 100,000 tons per year (lower than the average obtaining before the rise to 250,000 tons in 1934). Demand began to recover in the years 1935 and 1936, largely on rearmament programmes, and prices were held in a steady and unspectacular rise. Production and export quotas were progressively increased and at around £35 per ton for standard, it began to appear as though equilibrium had been achieved at last.

But nothing remains static to the point of permanent equipoise in a world market in raw materials. In 1936 and early in 1937 there came one of those commodity booms which prove so difficult to attribute to any particular cause, and speculators on the bull tack came on to the market in some numbers. Once again prices started advancing, and once again the cartel was too slow in reacting to check the rise by increasing quotas; consumers predictably began to buy before the market rose too far against them. In March 1937 standard stood at £78 5s 0d.

By the time cartel quotas had been raised, and production increased to new levels, the buying boom was already ended. An unnecessary surplus situation had once more been brought about by the attempt (albeit a well-intentioned one) at control of the market in the teeth of supply and demand forces. Prices fell to about £40 per ton, and both production and export quotas were duly reduced once more. And, once more, too late to save the situation.

The copper market on the LME since the Second World War.

Copper was the last of the four major metals to be returned to free market trading by the British Government after the war. Dealings actually recommenced on 5 August 1953 (and the market almost at

43

once went into a backwardation, as its reopening coincided with a shortage of supplies).

The post war scene in the world copper trade showed the main sources of production as Canada, Chile, the USA, the USSR, Zaire (Congo) and Zambia. New sources are, however, coming on stream at not infrequent intervals, and the Philippines and Bougainville are amongst these. Of the consuming countries Japan and West Germany emerged strongly as leading importers and refiners, whilst in the United States and the Russian bloc domestic production and consumption continue roughly to match each other.

The copper market continued to fluctuate: first downwards with the general running-down of the war machines of the belligerents; and later strongly upwards as industry (and notably the automobile industry) began to make heavy inroads on available supplies. As before, certain of the major producers began to look to fixed prices as a means of stabilising the market, and in 1955 the RST group initiated their own producer price to their customers: to be adjusted at intervals according to circumstances. (The other African Commonwealth producer, Anglo American, continued to base its prices on the LME.) But RST reverted to pricing on the LME after a couple of years, and the next move towards a producer or cartel price (outside the USA) was not to take place until 1961, when certain of the major producing countries established an agreed selling price of £234 per ton.

Before reviewing the progress of this latest attempt at a fixed-price system, it is worth noting that shortly before this time, Japan came on to the scene for perhaps the first time in an international sense. In 1957 the Japanese Government permitted her nationals to make use of the LME for hedging purposes. Much aptitude was shown by Japanese industry in this field and it was not too long before a more direct connexion was established. More than one LME member company now has a measure of Japanese shareholding, and the Japan Metal Centre was set up in London some few years ago as a further link.

To return to the producer price operation initiated in 1961, the countries participating were the African producers with Chile – but for various reasons their number excluded the United States, Canada and the USSR. The price rose from its original £234 by relatively easy stages to £336 in January 1966. This time, the price was proving to have been pegged too low – no doubt from concern regarding substitution for copper in various applications, notably by aluminium in the electrical field – and first Zambia and then Chile were persuaded to break away from the system. After a brief attempt at maintaining a producer price well in excess of that which had been the order of the day, Chile joined Zambia in the summer of 1966 in pricing on the LME three months quotation. Thereafter the LME became once more the medium, though the cash price was in a short time substituted for three months as the datum.

The three-tier copper contract on the LME.
With an eye to the ever-present need to keep the conditions of the contracts abreast of the needs of the industry, the LME came to a somewhat momentous decision: to break the standard copper contract down into components and give each of these the status of a contract in its own right. One overall norm for copper was no longer adequate; and though a system of discounts was a possibility it was felt that the divergence in end-uses and consequent different grades now sought by industry to meet these needs justified the introduction of multiple contracts. Accordingly, dealings in standard copper for three months ceased at the beginning of July 1963, with the contract thus phased-out at the end of September in that year.

In place of the standard contract there were instituted three separate contracts: for wirebars, cathodes (electro) and for fire-refined copper. Requirements for each were set so as to cater for the needs of one or other facet of the industry: with wirebars primarily intended (as the name implies) for wire-drawing and rod making, and cathodes for melting either to produce other shapes or for alloying. Of the three, fire-refined ceased to be priced officially each day after 1968. The wirebar contract was itself divided into separate categories for electrolytic and high conductivity fire refined (HCFR), which trades at a discount below the price for electro.

Introduction of the three-tier contract did not of itself prevent LME prices from rising well above those still fixed by the producers, and wirebars reached a high of £530 10s 0d in November 1964. They continued upward throughout 1965, and in April 1966 were priced at £787 10s 0d. It was at this point that the Chileans broke from the ranks of the producers' "club" and announced a selling price the equivalent of £496 sterling. This move was followed by the Zambian decision to revert to pricing their output on the much higher LME figure – though they based their quotations on three months rather than cash.

The divergence between the LME and the producer prices was

45

largely the outcome of the fact that the free (LME) market was at the time too narrow, and therefore too easily subject to pressure. In this instance, buyers were anxious to ensure their marginal needs via the LME and they were understandably not too concerned about the price paid for what was a relatively minor proportion of a total intake the bulk of which was bought at an artificially low producer price. Once the producers, with the exception of those in the USA, reverted to pricing on the LME this situation no longer obtained and LME prices reacted downwards to less extreme heights and closer to the true value in terms of world supply and demand. The Americans remained wedded to producers' fixed prices, but it should be borne in mind that conditions in their domestic market were quite unlike those outside it. The USA was roughly in balance as to production and demand, and over her domestic market there hung the tonnage in the strategic stockpile, which could be released in tranches by the General Services Administration (GSA) on approval of Congress.

In 1967 the picture changed once more, when a major (and in the event prolonged) strike by copper workers in the USA broke out after failure of the triennial wage negotiations. The free market price began to climb as buyers hurried to ensure supplies for themselves before production was too severely cut back or even stopped altogether. The position as far as the LME was concerned was aggravated by the desire of American consumers now to buy on the world market: their domestic sources of supply having by autumn been cut by as much as 90% of smelting and 70% of refining capacity. That summer also saw heavy forward buying on the market in anticipation of a devaluation of sterling (one of the then British Government's worst-kept secrets.) In the event, the pound sterling was devalued by some 14% on 18 November 1967, and the LME price of cash wirebars rose by roughly 10% from £502 to £556: indicating the extent of the discounting in advance which had taken place.

The strike in the USA continued. In early March 1968 record prices in excess of £840 were being offered for cash and a wide backwardation was ruling. But the signs were that the strike was at last coming to an end, as various individual plants settled fresh labour deals; at the end of the month cash wirebars had fallen to £620. The decline continued, and copper was to remain a largely quiet market in terms of price movements until the boom of 1973–74 when, for the first time ever, it was being traded at prices well into four figures. The highest official price being £1400 on 1 April 1974, with a backwardation of £191.

CIPEC and other outside bodies.

Since the middle of 1974 prices have declined to the point where (allowing for their being quoted in sterling – itself further devalued in terms of other currencies) the metal may have been selling at or below the cost of production in certain areas. This has given fresh stimulus to the four member countries of CIPEC (Intergovernmental Council of Copper Exporting Countries) in their efforts to find a formula for agreement on some kind of protection of prices. These countries are Chile, Peru, Zaire and Zambia. The organisation was set up in 1967, and to date it serves primarily – and constructively be it said – as a forum for the discussion and dissemination of views and information. A permanent staff is maintained at an office in Paris, and meetings at Ministerial level between members take place regularly at various centres: with guests and observers invited from outside CIPEC itself.

Precisely what the future holds for CIPEC is hard to forecast, but it seems moderately clear that this particular producer organisation (to date lacking members from the USA, Canada or the USSR amongst the major producing countries) is pursuing a more cautious line than its predecessors.

Other bodies, notably UNCTAD, have from time to time exercised themselves on the subject, but for the most part such concern has been with commodities or raw materials in general rather than with metals *per se*. Since copper is not a native product of any of the EEC members save to some extent in Ireland, there are no tariffs or restrictions imposed by the Commission on primary copper: though the movements of most kinds of scrap metal is subject to various controls.

The future of the copper market on the LME.

It is moderately certain that there will continue to be some disparity of view between supporters of free market pricing and the protagonists of some form of control; in consequence there will no doubt continue to be a measure of dual pricing. Attempts at controlling prices by controlling the market in one way or another have all been signal failures, and it is unlikely – in view of the sheer size of the copper producing and consuming world – that any one, or any group of interests will again be in a position seriously to make a further attempt. This is no claim to perfection on the part of the LME. The pattern and the scope of its market in copper must continually be the subject of review from within, and it will surely change from time to time in order to remain abreast of conditions in world markets. Requirements as to the actual grades and shapes of metal deliverable against the LME contracts must be such as to maintain that elusive balance between a "universal" hedging medium and a type of material suitable in every way for this or that different end-use. The possibility of a longer-term contract to meet the hedging needs of those trading in physical metal against 12 months supply contracts is also a subject for examination and discussion. That the contract has survived for the space of all but 100 years with only four major changes in that time goes a long way towards justifying the Exchange's claim as to its suitability to its purpose.

5

Tin and the Tin Contracts

To a great extent, copper and tin have a degree of affinity in the context of the LME. Both are historically very old metals, and both were the subject of the Exchange's first official contracts. This said, it is the points of divergence between the two metals that are of most direct concern. The first of these points of difference lies in the world supply situation for each metal. Whilst copper is naturally distributed in the earth on a more or less global scale (and is now known to occur under the sea in the manganese-copper-cobalt nodules) the areas where tin is mined or dredged are few in comparison with copper. In the early years of the LME supplies of tin were limited first to English, then to Straits and Australian and later to production from the Dutch East Indies. This narrowness of sources of supply is to an extent aggravated by the small proportion of total supplies which are recycled as secondary metal from recoveries of scrap.

A review of the history of the tin market on the LME will bring to light fresh divergencies between this and the other metals – notably in the overall marketing sphere – and these matters will be looked at in their own context in the ensuing pages.

Early history.
The amalgamation of tin and copper to make bronze can be said to date from circa 3000 BC, and Cornish production itself dates at least as far back as the first millennium BC. The trading voyages of the Phoenicians from what is now Tunisia to Britain are well authenticated, and it is plain that this was already an established trade long

before Julius Caesar's first expedition to Britain. It might well have been at least partly on account of knowledge of this profitable trade that the Romans came northwards at all and away from the area they already dominated.

Cornish tin, which of recent years has enjoyed a renewal of productive effort, was in mediaeval times associated with the Lamb and Flag brand mark. This constituted both a warranty as to purity and a confirmation that the King's dues had been met. The lamb carrying the flag is the emblem of the Knights Templar (who were the founders of the Inns of Court – Inner and Middle Temple – in London) and of the Knights Hospitaller, who possessed of the Norman and early Plantagenet Kings of England certain rights as to the sale of refined tin. For liturgical reasons, the brand mark was not universally acceptable – notably in Muslim countries – and after it had also been taken up by certain continental refiners it ceased to represent an exclusive trademark.

The importance to England of the production and trade in tin was reflected in the Charters granted by the Crown to the Stannaries, which gave a quite real measure of autonomy to certain towns in Cornwall, Devon and Somerset. (The curious history of the importance of tin to mediaeval and Tudor England is a study in itself, but is unfortunately out of place in the present context.) With the growth of London as a trading and financial centre, the influence of the Stannary towns declined, and control of the tin market passed into the hands of the Worshipful Company of Pewterers. It remained thus until the nineteenth century, when control was once more with the Cornish smelters and their agents. Marketing was by consignment of block tin from Cornwall to users or merchants in Bristol, Birmingham and London. Export was largely by way of London and Bristol merchants and the ubiquitous East India Company.

(In the latter part of the nineteenth century, exports and re-exports of tin amounted from a half to approximately three-quarters of home consumption.)

At this time, the import of tin from the East – the other major area of production – was inhibited by the imposition of a duty of no less than 60% *ad valorem*. In fact the average of imports between 1815 and 1830 amounted to only some 160 tons a year. By virtue of the *Warehousing Act* of 1823 it became possible to import and then re-export both tin and copper without attracting this extremely burdensome duty, and in consequence a brisk *entrepôt* trade in Australian and Straits tin was built up with the Continent of Europe. The higher purity of these brands, and their desirability in certain applications led to repeated approaches to the Government by the tinplaters in Wales, and eventually to a progressive dimunition of the tariff and to the birth of a significant import business in Eastern tin. As these uses of high-purity tin grew in volume, and notable amongst them was the expansion of the tinplating industry for which higher purity metal is essential, consumption of tin within the United Kingdom rose from some 6600 tons in 1860 to more than double that figure by 1875. By this time too, actual import of block tin was roughly double the re-export figure: indicating a very considerable domestic market within the UK. The English merchants meanwhile had established a dominant position in the world tin trade: accounting then for some 50% of world production. Only the market in Amsterdam holding periodic auctions of banka and billiton tin offered any serious rivalry.

The early LME tin contracts.
The contracts for tin on the LME originated in the same epoch as those for copper, and initially they appear to have taken much the same form as to deliveries and prompts. Alterations to the contracts in the light of experience were made from time to time, but in the case of tin the need was not so much to cater for a swiftly developing consumer demand as to safeguard the market from periodic squeezes. Total world supply of tin was not large, and stocks of the metal were often sufficiently low as to allow some manipulation of the market.

From the outset, the tin contracts were in units of five tons as opposed to 25 tons for the other base metals, and catered for delivery (in London only) of warrants in this amount.

Good merchantable quality (GMQ).
In 1891 the early contracts were superseded by a single GMQ contract. By permitting only the delivery of Australian and Straits tin however, this contract was to prove too narrow for hedging purposes even though it met the needs of those seeking physical deliveries.

Mixed tin.
In 1897 therefore, a second contract for mixed tin was introduced which included banka and billiton tin as good delivery. The effect of this move was that GMQ remained the chief delivery contract whilst hedging was largely done on mixed.

The addition to the range of the brands deliverable against the

51

mixed tin contract was unfortunately not enough to prevent the establishment from time to time of corners in what was, by comparison with copper, a relatively narrow market. (One particular firm, Messrs Ricard and Freiwald, became adept at obtaining control of nearby supplies and in so doing achieving a momentary hold over the market.)

The Committee were in due course approached with a view to their taking steps to prevent or at least inhibit such manipulation of the tin market. This taxed them with the difficult choice of allowing complete freedom in dealings on the market – one of the most basic principles of the LME – or of restricting any dealings which might be held to be endangering the market's equilibrium. In the event, the Committee opted for the latter course, as much to preserve the Exchange's reputation in the eyes of the world as for any other reason, and a new rule was adopted in 1899. This rule gave the Committee the right to release members from their market commitments to deliver warrants against outstanding contracts where it had been established that an "Oppressive Corner" was in being. Under this rule, prompts could be extended or effected at a predetermined settlement price. Unfortunately, in practice the rule was not altogether effective as at first framed, since it could then only be invoked at the behest of 12 members; in 1911 the Committee were authorised to invoke it on their own initiative. The rule still stands in the current Rules and Regulations as Contract Rule "H", and it gives the Committee the power if they think a corner is being established to "investigate the matter and to take whatever action it considers proper to restore equilibrium between supply and demand . . . " Practice is never as easy nor as precise as theory however, and the risk of being held to be oppressing one or more members to the benefit of others is a severe deterrent to the taking of any such drastic action. In actual fact, operation of the rule is by way of a quiet word with the offender in the majority of the infrequent cases of its being invoked at all.

The Committee still looked towards broadening the scope of the contract as the best means of achieving a more truly representative market. To this end, they were in 1911 considering admission as good delivery of English ingot, Chinese and German tin at seller's option, but the proposal was resisted by those members who represented consumers. These latter argued that the admission of inferior grades would worsen the position by driving users towards direct dealings with producers and so bypassing the LME – an argument which, with the benefit of hindsight, can be said to have had a lot of merit.

The standard tin contract.
This was introduced in 1912, in the face of strong opposition, in a further attempt to solve the intractable problem of supplies in a narrow market. Under this contract, sellers might deliver Class A tin of Australian or Straits origin, or refined tin assaying not less than 99.75 % Sn. Class B tin was the alternative – and the innovation – in that it included common tin from English and other suppliers assaying down to a permitted minimum of 99 % Sn. This latter was to be deliverable at a discount of £7 below the contract price.

Opposition to the new contract reached the point where some members refused to trade in it and confined their activities to GMQ; the difficulty was only partly resolved by the introduction in 1913 of a CIF contract for certain named grades, which were sold at buyer's option on shipment terms. The effect of these attempts at rationalising the market were to drive the greater part of physical trading away from the Ring, which became a hedging and from time to time a speculative medium.

All in all, the tin market on the LME was very volatile, and very prone to distortion during these years leading up to the First World War. Prices could range in the course of one year from a high of £200 to a low of £115, and from £233 to £169. All too easily understandable in a narrow market with insufficient geographical (and economic) spread as to its sources of supply. Malayan prices tended to fluctuate widely, and they were those on which exports from the East were priced. Sales of banka in Amsterdam were periodic, and resulted in periodic surges of supply in the West. The market was in fact passing through an unhappy phase of great vulnerability, and was the subject of more than one cornering attempt by numerous syndicates: of which Secretan has already been noted in connexion with copper. In 1888 the Secretan syndicate withdrew from the tin market (they were to hold out a little longer in copper), and prices in London promptly fell from £166 on 27 April to £80 on 4 May in that year.

As to the standard contract itself, further changes have been made in the continuing effort to maintain a balance between a broad hedging contract and one which is sufficiently precise as to enable a consumer to take up the desired grade of actual metal against it. By the mid 1920s, there was enough physical demand for the Class B

53

brands to allow the discount on English tin to have been all but eliminated in dealings done outside the market. Accordingly, official discounts were reduced first to £5 in 1925, and 10 years later to £4. In 1935 also the minimum purity requirement was lowered from 99% Sn to 98.5%: in order to include the increasing volume of Chinese tin which was by then being traded both in the UK and America. There was a fixed discount of £7 in the case of this lower grade metal.

By 1958 the contract was amended once more, this time to exclude common tin. At this date, metal had to be either Class A1 (named brands, including English refined tin) or A2 being other tin of good merchantable quality assaying not less than 99.75%. Both A1 and A2 were deliverable at the contract price. Later still, the standard contract crystallised as to quality requirements: stipulating a purity of not less than 99.75% and that the metal be "of a brand approved by and registered with the Committee". The naming of individual brands on the contract had been discontinued.

The tin market between the world wars.
After closure during the war years, the market was reopened for trading in December 1918 – remarkably soon after the cessation of hostilities – and prices began to fall rapidly from the levels reached during the war. The decline was short-lived though; the inexorable pull of inflation and depreciating currency values soon had prices climbing again. The trend was steepened by an appreciable amount of speculative buying for investment. In February 1920 tin at £419 had already surpassed its highest wartime price level. Within months, the reaction had set in however, and in the early part of the following year tin had fallen as low as £148. In industrial terms, the market was far from healthy: worldwide trade depression combined with a huge surplus of metal (either in stockpiles or in the form of now redundant items of ordnance) brought conditions which could only prove highly disadvantageous to the producing side of the metals industry. At about this period, the American and Chilean producers collaborated to form the Copper Export Association and a comparable operation in tin, the other major metal, was to be expected.

The Bandoeng Pool.
In December 1920, the governments of the Dutch East Indies and of Malaya formed the Bandoeng Pool, with the intention of buying-up surplus tin and so taking it off the market. During 1921 the pool did

actually purchase some 19,000 tons; the decline in prices was reduced if not altogether halted, and this with only minor reductions in current production capacity.

Other influences were at work on prices, however, and the years before the return to the Gold Standard in 1925 were times of extreme currency fluctuations. The German Mark after reaching unplumbed depths collapsed in 1922 at 50 billion Marks per pound sterling, and even after the stabilisation of the Mark in 1924 there were fresh fears for the French franc. Speculators, or indeed anyone with money to husband invested heavily in metals, or used the purchase and sale of metals or other commodities as a means for the transfer of paper money.

After these rather hectic years, comparative monetary stability was achieved with a general return to gold; this process being aided by the strengthening of the American economy, and the emergence in the USA of an industrial boom. (Unfortunately, these hopeful signs were not so manifest in Europe, with the United Kingdom, as an example, plunged into depression and a number of major strikes.) However, the international climate did become such that the Copper Export Association was wound up in 1924, and in the previous year the partners in the Bandoeng Pool began disposing of their stocks. This was carried out against a rising market in which consumption was now beginning to outrun production. So much so that when the disposals were completed in 1924 there was revealed the alleged "tin famine" – exaggerated perhaps, but real enough to bring about sharp and, in the event, lasting increases in prices.

This shortage brought fresh capital into prospecting and producing ventures. New mines and dredges were developed in Indo-China and Malaya and – significantly enough – in Nigeria, thus further demonstrating the extent of mineral reserves in the African continent. Mine output figures (overall) rose from 126,000 tons in 1923 to 196,000 in 1929, but by then signs were apparent of over-production, and prices started to fall in sympathy. Voices began to be heard within the industry asking once again for some form of control of output in order to bolster up sagging prices. (In fact, the Anglo Oriental Corporation had already secretly withheld some of its production from the market with this aim in view.) The continuing decline in consumption in the years of the great depression made some form of restraint on production desirable if not actually essential.

The Tin Producers Association had been formed in 1929, largely as a forum for discussion, and this body now started endeavouring to persuade its members to restrict their own output on a voluntary basis. There was some response – which gave a measure of encouragement – but not sufficient seriously to assist in maintaining prices in the face of continuing oversupply. By the end of 1930, world tin stocks stood at 47,000 tons and the price was down to £112.

The International Tin Restriction Scheme.
This was set up in 1931, and was organised at government level by the major producing countries, with the declared object of obtaining "a fair and reasonable relation between production and consumption . . . (in order to) . . . prevent rapid and severe oscillations in price". The scheme was to be worked according to a formula: under which each member country would be allotted a standard tonnage, and its production based on a percentage quota of this amount. Quotas, which could be varied each quarter, were enforceable by the member governments. The membership of the schemes covered some 90% of world production capacity, with only China and the Congo as absentees amongst the larger producers.

The prospects for such a scheme were no doubt brighter in tin than in the other non-ferrous metals. There was (and remains) a far smaller element of scrap in tin than in copper and lead, for example; and consumers in the main bought or stayed their hands more on current industrial conditions than on account of fluctuations in prices on the market.

The International Tin Committee was established as the governing body for the scheme, and commenced operations in March 1931. For the first year of operations, results were not very encouraging. However, the quotas were reduced in 1932 to one third only of the standard tonnages, and prices began to turn upwards once more. Success fed upon success as stocks contracted – aided by the general increase in consumption of tin by industry – and prices in fact reached the comforting figure of £230 per ton by the end of 1933. This from a level of £118 in 1931 – the first year of the scheme's operation.

The Tin Buffer Pool.
The scheme was reinstated in 1934 for a further three-year period; that year quotas were increased yet remained below consumption with stocks declining to less than 20,000 tons. The average price was held at £230. In point of fact, an artificial shortage had been brought into being. Observing this, the International Tin Committee took the decision to establish a buffer pool of tin which could itself be ex-

panded or contracted as a means of effecting a finer and more rapidly responsive adjustment than the somewhat crude method of restrictions on production. In a falling market the pool would buy surplus metal, which it would be in a position to sell on the market once more in case rising consumption (or speculative activity) were seen to be forcing prices too high.

The proposal to set up the buffer pool was not at the time universally welcomed. There were many who felt that the position had been brought sufficiently under control for it to have been an unnecessary subtlety. There were also objections to maintaining the price as high as £230 per ton: such a figure being held to be an encouragement to the continuance of high-cost production (being now profitable at such price levels) at the expense of further development of lower-cost and arguably more efficient operations. Consumers naturally saw the development as yet another strengthening of the producers' already close hold on the market: to no discernible benefit to themselves or their interests.

The reaction of the LME was both hostile and swift. Alarmed at the deleterious effect on the market of the transfer of all power of decision to the Buffer Pool Manager of the International Tin Committee, the Board of the Exchange sent a sharp protest to the British Colonial Office, in which they roundly condemned the whole concept as being against the interests of a free and open market.

Notwithstanding these hostile reactions, the pool was formally established in July 1934: supplies going directly into it from members of the International Tin Agreement. The pool started life therefore with some 8000 tons of tin to its name. Members of the agreement meanwhile continued to look kindly on the formation of "private" stock pools, and the International Tin Committee continued to buy metal from all comers when the market price fell below £230. The buffer pool itself did not trade in its early months, as quotas were still restricted to 40% of standard tonnages and by the end of 1934 world stocks were down to only 19,000 tons.

The situation grew progressively more acute in the following year. Supplies of visible tin in the United Kingdom fell to "starvation" levels with the inescapable result that a wide backwardation appeared. In fact, the shortage of tin for delivery had the effect of virtually stopping the LME from functioning at all: the backwardation made hedging an impossible business, and deliveries to and from the market were reduced to a trickle. (An extensive backwardation invariably has this unfortunate effect on hedging, since covering-in places the

57

hedger at the mercy of the "back".) Both the LME and the consuming and merchant trades continued to protest, without at the time persuading the International Tin Committee to increase supplies to the market. By way of a demonstration of their disapproval and frustration, it is reported that the LME dealers walked out of the tin Ring on one occasion!

It would appear that communications at the time between the ITC and the Exchange could not have been of the best. The ITC maintained that the LME was "a playground for both bulls and bears", and that sales of cash tin on the market were nothing more than the result of bear speculation. In perspective, it would seem less than likely that a speculator in such market conditions would put himself in the position of an uncovered bear: the sales were almost certainly genuine hedging. However, the ITC were not convinced. The tin market on the LME remained in considerable disarray throughout 1935. On 22 July for example, bidders in the Ring for cash tin pushed their bids up from £236 to £245 without attracting a single seller. Further protests were made to Whitehall: to be countered by the rather baffling rejoinder that (though Britain was a member of the ITC) HM Government accepted no responsibility for the policy of the manager of the buffer pool. Reassurances were however given – apparently contradicting the disclaimer – that the pool would be so administered as not to interfere with the normal workings of the Exchange. But stocks of tin in Liverpool and London remained at precariously low levels (to a low, in November, of 300 tons as compared with a usual average of around 5000 tons), and the wide backwardation continued.

The ITC did, however, respond to the situation they had themselves largely created by raising production quotas twice in the course of 1935 – ultimately to 90% of the standard tonnages. In the following year, stocks in the United Kingdom began to assume less desperate levels and the Exchange responded with a narrowing backwardation. However, 1936 continued on an unsettled course. There were uncertainties about the likely renewal of the scheme (and what form it might take), there were difficulties over the continued membership of Thailand, and these were reflected in widely fluctuating prices after a sharp break that summer. The third International Tin Agreement was in fact signed at the end of 1936 with prices once more in excess of £230.

In the following year, 1937, world trade was again on the ascendant, and the combined requirements of a considerable boom and heavy rearmament programmes brought huge increases in demand. In March, prices touched £311, the buffer pool was exhausted of tin and production quotas were duly raised as high as 110% of the standard tonnages. In the closing months of the year there was a general decline in production which was to continue throughout 1938. At the time, there was a recession in the USA, and this was to prove the major influence on the market. Prices again began to waver and then to fall: eventually to below £200 per ton. The market was further upset that year by a spate of rumours of the formation of a new buffer pool.

The second Tin Buffer Pool was brought into operation in June 1938. Once again, it was stocked initially by tin provided by members of the agreement rather than by purchases in the market. The innovation on this occasion was the establishment of the concept of a range of prices which would dictate the limits of permitted activity on the part of the manager. In this instance, he might sell or buy in order to contain prices within the band £200 to £230 per ton. Again, there was outspoken opposition to the scheme, including the accusation of adding price-fixing (within narrow limits) to the existing catalogue of producer-controlled restrictions to a free market. Indeed, since the London price at the time was but £188 it did appear that the producers were merely seeking protection for themselves at the expense of consumers. Speculators too foresaw the possibility of a rise in price and started their operation with this in view; and numerous private "pools" were set up by purely speculative interests.

During the year production quotas were again reduced, with the consequence that supplies became short once more. However, as prices rose to £230 in 1939 the buffer pool accordingly began to offer tin to the market. But the Second World War was imminent: demand rose strongly and the UK Government itself intervened to peg the London price at a maximum of £230, and to introduce a system of export licensing in order to conserve strategic supplies. For a time, the free market shifted to New York, and prices there rose from the equivalent of £229 per ton in August to £331 in the following month. By the end of August 1939 the buffer stock was virtually exhausted, production quotas were increased, and any serious attempt at control over the market was placed in abeyance. With the removal in December of the official price ceiling in the UK, London prices (once more free) averaged around £249.

These attempts at control appeared to have suffered from many of the shortcomings which afflicted similar operations in copper, and to have brought in their train very comparable side effects. What was to emerge and develop in the years after the war?

The tin market on the LME since the Second World War.

Being primarily a sterling commodity, tin did not present the same exchange problems as did the markets in the other metals. In addition, production of tin in the early post-war years was already running ahead of consumption, thus refuting any argument for the continuation of Government rather than free market buying. There remained some risk of loss of foreign exchange resulting from commodity "shunting", but such losses could only occur where there existed unofficial markets in transferable sterling which was offered at a discount below official parity. This risk was greatly reduced by the devaluation of the pound sterling in September 1949.

At the end of September the UK Government announced the termination of bulk purchasing contracts for tin, and with the exception of the disposal of remaining stocks, Government intervention in the market could cease. Accordingly, 15 November 1949 saw the reopening of the tin market: the first of the LME markets to be freed after the end of the war.

The Bank of England Metals Scheme.

Dealings still had to be accommodated within the framework of exchange control regulations and requirements however, and in order to ensure this, arrangements were worked out by the Bank of England and the Committee of the LME acting in close co-operation. The general tenor of these arrangements is covered on later pages and the scheme is mentioned here in order merely to establish its place in the chronological order of developments.

Since rubber was the only other London Commodity market already re-opened, the recommencement of tin dealings on the LME excited much interest and comment in business circles worldwide. Its success or otherwise was seen to be a reliable indicator of the likely success of other markets, and indeed, of the concept of free markets generally in the economic world now emerging. In all, the successful re-opening, after a long period of scrupulously careful preparation, of the first of its markets was a very real fillip to the whole image and morale of the LME.

One major problem remaining was how best to ensure the orderly disposal of the country's strategic stocks of tin? The Committee of the LME were as one in the opinion that any such disposals should be done by way of sales in the market, on the standard contract. It was proposed that one broker be charged with responsibility for the sales and by agreement with the Ministry of Supply, Mr J. D. Wolff (Chairman of the Committee) was appointed in this capacity. A nice touch was the agreement within the Exchange that commissions received be pooled for sharing equally amongst the Ring members! To start with, the market was almost wholly dependent upon the "Government Broker" for its chips in terms of cash metal, and balanced stocks were only built up with some difficulty as other warrants began to make their appearance. Prices at the outset fell noticeably, indicating an over-valuation of tin in the years without a free market. The Ministry's last official quotation had been £750, but by 25 November – 10 days after the market re-opened –standard had fallen to £642 10s 0d cash, and at year's end to barely £600. At first there was a considerable backwardation as the direct reflection of a lack of stocks: but this had given way to a narrow contango in March 1950 as conditions became more stable and stocks were being built up. All was indeed proceeding very smoothly, until the outbreak of hostilities in Korea in June 1950. Immediately, buying developed on a very large scale and an acute shortage was seen to be approaching very rapidly. Fears were based on two main grounds: first the general human tendency to stockpile in time of crisis, and secondly quite well founded fears of a spread of hostilities severely disrupting shipping to and from the East and the transit of such supplies as remained on offer. The United States led the way with massive purchases for her own stockpile, and other nations followed suit: there was also the predictable scramble by speculators to come into what was now a rapidly rising market.

The market in fact rose in an unprecedented manner. From averaging around £600 per ton from the start of dealings until early 1950, cash tin reached £800 by mid-August and £1300 in November. On 14 February the high point was reached of no less than £1615 per ton, with three months at a considerable backwardation. A far cry from the immediately pre-war support price of £200–£300. An unfortunate effect of this heavy buying by relatively few purchasers was the dependence of others on rumours of their intentions and forthcoming activities, and the consequent erratic behaviour of the market – with daily fluctuations as great as £100. In the UK the Ministry of Supply became alarmed at the shortage of stocks, and announced in August that it could no longer be depended upon as a willing seller of cash. However, stocks on warrant totalled only a nominal 100 tons, shipments from the East were, in the event, gravely disrupted and the Ministry was compelled to make sales from time to time in order to keep the market open at all. This it did on condition that members themselves operated a self-imposed ban on sales for export. The seemingly relentless upward pressure on prices under these conditions was the subject of much worried discussion and negotiation, as government and other agencies sought some form of agreement to limit what had degenerated into a scramble for supplies at virtually any price. The rise could only be, and in the event was, stopped by the removal of its root cause. The by now enormous cost of stockpiling finally persuaded Congress in the United States to stage a dramatic alteration of course. In a report, a Committee of Congress has accused producers of "gouging" the US taxpayers by failing to increase output to meet vastly increased demand. (As this increase in demand could be said to be exceptional, and in all probabillity of limited duration, it is rather hard to see the justice of such an accusation. What would have happened later to the surplus capacity which might thus have been brought on stream?) The US Administration then decided to discontinue stockpile purchases until prices had fallen "to a reasonable level". In March, the Reconstruction Finance Corporation was authorised as the sole importer into the USA, and even usual commercial purchases were suspended on the grounds that producers were asking too much for their metal or concentrates. Controls were at the same time placed upon consumption within the US.

Tin now found itself in surplus once more, and prices in London fell almost as fast as they had risen: falling to £867 in July 1951. Throughout this whole cycle, the LME traded without interruption or embarrassment to any member. For the ensuing two years, and no doubt to the relief of those concerned, the tin market passed through a period of quite remarkable tranquillity. Average prices in fact varied between a minimum of £948 and a maximum of £984 in the period January 1952 to March 1953. This even tenor of prices was not the outcome solely of free-market dealing however. The RFC had entered into fixed price purchasing agreements with the governments of the Congo, Indonesia and the United Kingdom, and this enabled it to be a seller at a consistent £964 (121.5 cents per lb). Originally a floor price, the figure became the ceiling price after August 1952 when normal commercial imports into the USA were resumed. London prices continued to follow the RFC as supplies from other sources were still insufficient to meet demand, which had perforce to lean heavily on RFC sales. The situation persisted until early 1953, when prices started again to break. The RFC's purchasing contract was shortly to terminate and it was felt that a surplus would result; in addition there was a slackening of international tensions with the cessation of hostilities in Korea. In July 1953 the London price fell to £567. Although in retrospect these two years had been years of stability as to prices in London, this very stability had impeded the equally necessary hedging and speculative activity on the market.

There had also been a resuscitation of commodity shunting activity due to the weakness of transferable sterling. Merchants on the Continent were able to take advantage of cheap transferable sterling rates and so buy tin in London and Singapore for sterling, sell it at "cut price" terms for US dollars in New York and still show a profit on the exchange conversion. It was intimated that some 30,000 tons of Straits tin found a home in the United States by this route: costing the United Kingdom some $80,000,000 in dollar reserves. At the request of the Bank of England, the Committee of the LME appealed to members to be chary of taking business from doubtful sources and in particular to check carefully any terms in contracts for "on-shipment" with clients outside the United Kingdom. At the same time, the authorities in Malaysia co-operated by requiring certificates from purchasers of Straits tin confirming that the material had been consumed in the country to which it had been consigned, and not "shipped-on".

The only real cure to this as to so many problems, however, could be the removal of its true cause: in this case the difference between official exchange rates for sterling and the unofficial rates. In early 1953 the Exchange Equalisation Account took the decision to support the exchange rate on dealings in overseas markets and thus keep it so close to the official rate that discount dealings were no longer profitable. Whilst this disparity in rates for sterling brought about technical disparities between tin prices in London, Singapore and New York (which were normally, and ought to be, in harmony), it also had an adverse effect on the business of the London dealers who were unable to take advantage of cheap sterling rates in order to meet competition in the New York market as to the dollar price there.

The Penang market – "The East".
Before considering the recent history of tin on the LME in the con-

text of the new International Tin Agreement, a brief word on the Penang market or "the East" as it is known. Sales take place each day in Penang of metal produced by the Straits Trading Company, the Eastern Smelting Company and certain other local interests. The method used is more akin to the "fix" on the London Bullion Markets than to the LME open outcry system or to an auction in the traditional sense.

Bids are put in by the buyers and then considered in the light of the daily intake of ore. The price is usually announced at midday, based on the bids themselves and the tonnage available, in such a way that normally the day's tonnage is distributed between the bidders at the official price for the day.

Should the bids exceed the tonnage for disposal on any day, the allocation to bidders is rationed, and should the declared price on any day be higher than certain of the bids, the entire tonnage need not be disposed of. Metal is sold ex-smelter as a rule for delivery within 60 days. It is important to note that the East is a market in physical tin only, that no futures are traded and, therefore, hedging is not possible on the Penang market.

The International Tin Agreements: 1956 to the present.
The first International Tin Agreement was drawn up in 1956 under the auspices of the United Nations and after preliminary work by the International Tin Study Group. It was to be effective for five years. On this occasion, and for the first time, consuming countries as well as producers were represented in the International Tin Council. For the first time also, to the old "range" of the pre-war buffer pools was added the further sophistication of three "ranges" between the floor and the ceiling price. Above the ceiling price the buffer stock manager was obliged to sell and between the ceiling and the lower limit of the upper range he might sell at his own discretion. In the neutral range he was not permitted to operate, could buy in the lower range, and must buy at or below the floor price. All prices were based on the LME in London, and the buffer stock manager operated (as he still does) via LME members. The old "Government Broker" concept of the past was replaced by a system whereby the buffer stock manager operated through any member of his choice and spread his business as evenly as possible among them. (There is a story – probably apocryphal – that at first he took the names in alphabetical order. Thus if it became known or suspected that member "A" was the chosen instrument on any day, then it was a

safe assumption that "B" would be favoured next time the buffer stock manager came into the Market: his fellows in the Ring were then in a position to lie in wait for him – .)

Original signatories to the first ITA were: Bolivia, Congo, Indonesia, Malaya and Nigeria (as producers), and Australia, Belgium, Canada, Denmark, Equador, France, India, Netherlands, Spain and the UK. Notable absentees were the USA, Russia and Federal Germany.

As an important producer, Thailand was a significant later signatory during the course of the first agreement.

The first agreement gave the ITC the right to deal with any stockpile held in member countries, though the largest of these by far – being the American – was excluded from the agreement. Declining world consumption, and the large tonnage in the US stockpile overhanging the market in fact brought about the ITA's first crisis, in 1958. In spite of restrictions on exports by members of the agreement the price fell below the floor of £730 and the buffer stock was unable financially to continue support buying. For a time dealings in tin on the LME were suspended.

The following year the position was radically altered, and the buffer stock as a seller found itself in acute danger this time of running out of tin.

The Second ITA came into being in 1961, and on this occasion the buffer stock contributions from members were in cash only, and not in physical metal. All prices in the range were raised.

At this point, it is necessary to introduce the American General Services Administration (the GSA) This body controls the US stock-. piles of all strategic raw materials necessary to the defence and to the economic requirements of the USA. The GSA has from time to time operated to alleviate a general shortage of any of these materials, by releasing on to the market tonnages surplus to America's own needs. In the 1960s the tin stockpile was greatly in excess of immediate (or immediately foreseeable) US requirements – partly as a consequence of the buying campaign mounted by the RFC during the Korean crisis. Partly to ease world shortages, but also in order to ease any strains on the US's own foreign exchange due to imports by US consumers, the GSA has been concerned to release as much as possible of its stockpiled material. Releases of tin, for example, amounted to no fewer than 28,994 tons in 1964 – equal to five weeks of the average world total consumption of tin.

Sales were priced on a formula taking in the average LME and

Penang sellers prices over a period, though the GSA reserved to itself the right to sell at what it described as "a proper market bid". Despite genuine efforts on the part of the GSA to make weekly sales ex-stockpile, prices continued to rise in the early years of the second ITA until in April 1963 the price went through the buffer stock's ceiling. This was to a large extent attributable to new Russian buying to meet a possible shortfall in Indonesian deliveries – no doubt on account of the situation in Vietnam. On 28 November in that year, cash again reached the buffer stock manager's "must sell" figure of £965, and the buffer stock found itself exhausted of tin.

A meeting between representatives of the US Administration and of the ITC was held in Washington in November 1963, resulting in a reassurance from the United States as to their "long term disposal programme". But notwithstanding, the shortage persisted: with cash tin in excess of £1000 per ton by the end of the year. The year 1964 saw much the same pattern repeating itself, especially as the Vietnam crisis had now developed into a war situation with the USA heavily involved. The London price fluctuated from a low of £1022 in March, and reached its high to date, at £1714 in October 1964. The ITA once more revised its prices, with the floor at £1000 and ceiling at £1200. The following year was again a period of wide fluctuation in price, from £1191 in January (after falling back from the previous October's high), to a peak of £1622 at the year's end.

The third ITA was established in 1966, and the price range was now: floor £1100, middle range from £1200 to £1300 and ceiling £1400 (the ranges between floor and ceiling and middle range being the "may buy" and "may sell" areas, respectively).

In the third ITA the buffer stock was established again wholly in cash: contributions amounting to the equivalent of 10,000 tons at a notional price of £1000 per ton. A further improvement as to flexibility was the power given to the Council to impose export quota limits on producing countries should the buffer stock manager have found it necessary to purchase 5000 tons or more. Now, however, the GSA had again emerged as a seller and this fact, coupled with an increase in productive capacity encouraged by earlier high prices was sufficient to restrain prices to below £1230. Indeed, a surplus of tin was once more a possibility.

The first three-quarters of 1967 continued along the same trend, with a surplus beginning to be in evidence. The LME price was steady for the most part around £1200 at which levels it was possible for the Buffer Stock Manager to buy, though it is not known to what extent he did so – if at all. The Arab-Israeli "Seven Days War" in June did not, in the event, have much effect on prices, and the next jolt was in November of that year.

Sterling devaluation.

In November 1967 the pound sterling was devalued by 14%. The ITC adjusted prices to a new (and wider) range between a floor of £1280 and a ceiling of £1630. The buffer stock manager was now a buyer and continued to support the Market until August of the following year: holding cash tin at or above a minimum of £1300. Consequent on this support programme, the buffer stock stood at over 7000 tons in January 1968 when a further call totalling £10,000,000 was made on producer members. The third ITA also provided for a standby bank credit of £10,000,000 should all or any of this extra money be required.

In 1969, the buffer stock manager was authorised to operate within the middle sector of the range (£1400 to £1515). He was a seller throughout the summer of that year, but by November his stocks had fallen to 5000 tons and with the price still rising. The ITC then agreed to hold these remaining stocks as reserves; and in December 1969 the price reached £1600. It seems that, excellent though the scheme was in concept and in execution, it could not go far enough and a basic buffer stock of 20,000 tons was quite inadequate. It is interesting to compare this with the American GSA stockpile which in 1968 stood at 257,000 tons. However much a non-member may genuinely seek to co-operate, his very existence as a holder of stocks of such magnitude must have an adverse effect on the International Buffer Pool.

The fourth ITA was established on 1 July 1971. The United States remained a "friendly outsider". Australia, then the world's fifth largest producer, rejoined as a producer member, and the ranks of the consumer members were also strengthened with the addition of the USSR and the German Federal Republic. This time, the International Monetary Fund agreed to provide support for contributions required from members; and the buffer stock manager was accorded far greater freedom in that he might now borrow and lend on the LME – thus enabling him to avail himself of the full gamut of the Exchange's facilities. The range was confirmed at £1650 ceiling down to £1350 floor prices. But the market in the latter half of 1971 was still generally overstocked, with the contango in July out to nearly £20. Most purchasers by this time were opting for higher-purity metal than the 99.75% LME standard tin. This produced a market differential between the LME and Penang prices, as the demand lay for high grade tin in Penang: despite availability of high grade via the LME at a modest premium over standard. LME prices then were averaging around £1450.

By late autumn the position was reached where the buffer stock manager was supporting the market at about £1390 per ton. He was probably holding some 4000 tons, which increased to 7000 tons by early 1972.

The high grade tin contract.

The LME standard contract was at this time losing some of its authority. A shortage of 99.75% tin had come about, chiefly due to the liquidation of one of the major UK smelters and in consequence a growing proportion of metal of higher purity was being traded against the standard contract at varying premiums. Considerable trade was also by-passing the LME altogether, and it was felt that the shortcomings of the one standard contract might be a contributory factor to this undesirable trend.

A sub-committee was set up to look into the matter, and their thinking at first took them towards a reversion to the erstwhile practice of naming the brands to be good delivery against the new contract.

Later, it was decided not to pursue this course, but to stipulate a purity of not less than 99.85% Sn and to invite the producers of the higher grades to offer their brands for registration under the new contract. The response from the producers was encouraging, and the buffer stock manager also voiced his support for the concept of a separate high grade tin contract. With this encouragement, the new contract was approved and instituted in August for prompts on and after 1 November 1974. After a somewhat hesitant start, with dealings in both contracts taken together in the same Ring, a pattern does now appear to be emerging and the premium for high grade over standard showing itself in official dealings – at any rate for forward dates. It remains to be seen how, or if, the two contracts do eventually show their individual paces; any development towards this will no doubt be followed closely by those with an interest in the establishment of a separate higher grade contract in zinc.

In many ways tin is the most subtle of the LME metals. The history of the various international agreements (for the most part at government level) is also an indication of its importance in the world scene. That these agreements have continued, and with more than a little real success in stabilising supply and demand, must go some way towards demonstrating that a workable combination of producer and consumer interests operating through a free and quite neutral pricing medium can be arrived at and made to work effectively.

6

Lead and Zinc

The situation as to lead and zinc on the LME is very different from that of the other metals. Both are found in some abundance in Europe and the mining and smelting of European ores contributes to a size-able overall production of refined metal. Britain herself was an ex-porter of lead in earlier times, though increasing industrialisation in the eighteenth and nineteenth centuries later reversed the picture, as had been the case with English tin. The main areas of British produc-tion were located in the Pennines (with Chesterfield as a marketing centre), the Mendips and the Welsh Mountains. After the Union of the two countries, Scottish output from Lanarkshire and the central Lowlands was added. Production from these mines was for the most part smelted locally, and shipments for exports sailed from Bristol, London, the Tyne and the South Wales ports.

Along with Germany and Spain – though a larger producer than either – the United Kingdom thus remained one of the world's leading producers of lead until the latter part of the nineteenth century. However, at this time the somewhat fragmented mining industry in the UK began to give way before continental competition, and in 1870 both Germany and Spain surpassed the British output of lead. Before the turn of the century the United States in her turn surpassed all others to become the world's premier producer. (At the same time, however, mining operations were getting under way in Australia and Mexico amongst other areas, and these countries too were in due course to become important centres of production.)

By the 1880s therefore, Britain was established as an importer of lead to the tune of some 100,000 tons per annum of pig and sheet and more than 16,000 tons of ore. Imports by that time already amounted to over three times her own domestic production. It is worth noting though that an *entrepôt* trade in lead was developing as well: in 1885 this onward business totalled almost 40,000 tons.

As to zinc (or spelter as it was known until after the First World War), production had largely been concentrated in Europe; and by the middle of the nineteenth century the region of Upper Silesia was the chief producing area. Smelting was for the most part carried out in Belgium and Germany, at first with European ores only, although later imported ores and concentrates were used as the industry grew rapidly to very large figures. The USA too was a producer of zinc, but being to a great extent self-supporting as to raw materials (with the exception of tin) her output was for the most part used in her own domestic consumption.

During the nineteenth century, both the production and the trade in zinc as they affected the LME were centred on, and largely controlled from the Continent. Commodity exchanges were in fact established in various European locations (and not only for dealings in metals): the Hamburg Metal Exchange being opened in 1910. This particular market achieved a considerable importance in dealings in lead and zinc in the relatively brief period before its closure in 1914. European exports to Britain were for the most part unloaded in Hull and in London. There was at the time but little *entrepôt* business in zinc, and market activity in London was almost exclusively confined to physical dealings by merchants in respect of UK consumption.

This predominance of Germany in the lead and zinc fields was to a very great extent attributable to the success of a few major enterprises: amongst them being Metallgesellschaft of Frankfurt. These organisations spread their interests widely both in terms of geography and of the various stages of production from mining through to marketing the refined metals. (Indeed, the whole Spanish mining industry was then very dependent on German investment.) Metallgesellschaft was later to build itself into a position of particular importance, and it is of more than passing interest to observe that this organisation – which was founded in the 1860s by the Merton brothers – is a Ring dealing member of the LME through its London company.

The LME and the contracts before the First World War.
Dealings in lead and zinc were for the most part confined to a

71

relatively few members, and were conducted outside the main Ring. This was not necessarily due to lack of interest in these metals but to the fact that they were not at the time (nor indeed for some years to come) sold on the basis of a transferable warehouse warrant giving title to a parcel of stocks in warehouse. It was not then possible to conduct hedging business in lead or zinc: deliveries were ex ship and for cash against bills of lading or delivery orders. There were wide variations in the purity of metal supplied, and this factor did not make the setting of a standard contract-unit of material any easier. The two factors combined to restrict almost entirely to physical dealings a market where as yet there was no formalised contract nor freely transferable documents of title such as were in use for dealings in copper and tin.

The Good Soft Pig Lead Contract was introduced in 1903 and was the outcome of much discussion in the endeavour to arrive at a formula which would make it feasible for lead to be bought and sold forward in the same way as tin and copper. The contract made no attempt to limit deliverable grades to a list of approved brands, as it was not felt necessary for consumers to be so specific in their choice of material. Warehouse warrants were still not used, and deliveries continued to be ex ship or ex wharf in the Thames between Nine Elms and Tilbury: the Port of London Authority area. Later, a system of discounts admitted deliveries further down-river.

An ex ship delivery, rather than one from stock already in warehouse, meant uncertainties as to completion dates. The new contract was in this sense more akin to those in use on the "soft" commodity markets in that it provided for a delivery month (rather than a prompt date) up to three months ahead. A further period of grace of 15 days was allowed to the seller, in the event of delayed arrival of ship,

With all its looseness, and consequent shortcomings as a really viable hedging medium, the new contract was a success. Indeed, it survived with surprisingly little change up to quite recent times.

A comparable contract for virgin spelter was introduced in 1915, with delivery points extended to include Liverpool (ex quay or ex warehouse) and Swansea. (FOR).

Producer cartels before the First World War.
The concentration of the lead and zinc industries in a relatively few areas (and in relatively few pairs of hands) made conditions much less unfavourable for the establishment of producer cartels than had been the case with either copper or tin. Outside the USA, which

72

being self-sufficient at the time was largely isolated from the rest of the world trade, the main smelters were located in Belgium and Germany and to a lesser degree in Britain and France. Ownership of many of these smelters furthermore was confined to a few organisations and the cartel "rationale" generally was both established and indeed encouraged in Germany.

Throughout the last decade of the nineteenth century there were repeated rumours in circulation as to a potential zinc cartel and they were sufficiently strong as to have an unsettling effect on prices. At the time, the industry was labouring under difficult conditions of low prices combined with high raw material costs: some form of co-operation on the part of the producers therefore appeared to be a strong possibility. In the event, however, the producers were unable to agree on a combined plan for restriction of output, the rumours began to be discounted and prices to recover. The notion of a producers' cartel was not revived until 1908 in fact, when the German industry approached groups in Belgium, Britain and France with the result that in 1909 the European Spelter Convention was set up.

The aim of the Convention was the control of production, and each producer member agreed to abide by a quota which would be reduced if stocks rose to more than 50,000 tons or the London price fell below £22 per ton. (There was no attempt made at actually fixing prices.) As happened with comparable cartels in other metals the Convention's early years appeared successful: to the extent of its renewal in 1911 for a further three years. (It is interesting to speculate on the exact cause and effect of these parallel situations. Would things have been otherwise had there been no cartel – since action was not in the event demanded of it – or did its very existence in some way and for a limited time so restrain disruptive forces as to maintain an orderly market almost in spite of itself?) In any case, the years 1911 and 1912 were happy ones for the European zinc producers, with a general expansion in trade and active markets.

In 1913 the Convention was put to the test for the first time. Early in that year consumption fell appreciably, production (inevitably, viewed with the benefit of hindsight), was reduced too late and stocks began to pile up. From £26 5s 0d in January the London price fell to £20 5s 0d in June 1913. When they were finally agreed and imposed, the restrictions on output were but reluctantly accepted by members of the Convention. Even had it not in fact been abandoned on the outbreak of war in August 1914, its future must already have been in doubt.

The Lead Smelters' Association was also set up in 1909, but followed a different pattern from that of the zinc cartel. In this instance, Metallgesellschaft were the prime movers – themselves controllers directly or indirectly of most of the German and other non-USA lead output. The company secured the co-operation of the major Belgian and Spanish producers in agreeing that the entire output of the cartel be marketed by Metallgesellschaft. This, therefore, was an operation along price-control rather than production-control lines, since Metallgesellschaft reckoned they would be able to sell metal to, or hold it back from the market in such a fashion as to preclude any undue fluctuations in price.

The weak American selling that had so bedevilled the zinc convention when prices generally were falling was more or less neutralised by the terms of an agreement with the American Smelting and Refining Company (Asarco). The only apparent danger therefore would have been stocks already independently held in Europe. In the event these stocks were largely eliminated over a period, independent producers gave no trouble and the average London price of good soft pig lead rose from £12 8s 0d in 1910 to £18 15s 0d in 1913. The Association was still enjoying its rosy first years when it too was closed down at the outbreak of war in 1914. What it might have achieved in the longer term (and in a less generally favourable market) must therefore remain a matter for conjecture.

The First World War.
The events which affected the LME both during and immediately after the First World War need to be considered in rather more detail in the context of lead and zinc than in that of the other metals. Germany represented a force of very considerable strength and influence where lead and zinc were concerned, and the way in which this situation developed both during and after hostilities has a bearing on the post-war LME which should not be overlooked.

The first reaction to the inevitability of war with Germany was the closure of the LME altogether; and this was done on 31 July 1914. The motivation appears to have been more a concern over possible disruption of supplies – Germany herself was after all the main adversary – and the fear of more general shortages due to disruption of shipping than any policy decision as to replacement of the metal trade by British Government purchasing agencies. The LME remained closed for some three months, and was reopened on 18 November 1914 after a brief spell of unofficial trading between members; and dealings at first were rather strictly confined. Lead and zinc imports from Germany and German occupied or controlled countries naturally ceased almost at once.

Whilst the position as to lead was not critical, that of supplies of zinc to Britain was difficult in the extreme. The UK smelting industry was not large – being only able to meet about a third of domestic requirements – and the country had come to rely very heavily on German and Belgian imports. There were by this time considerable supplies of ores and concentrates available in Australia which previously had for the most part been exported to Germany for smelting. Even after the German contracts were terminated therefore, the problem of ensuring adequate smelter capacity remained acute. By the end of 1915 zinc prices stood at three times their immediately pre-war levels, and it is thought probable that quite large speculative positions had been built up.

In consequence of these and other happenings, the British Government intervened to prevent "speculative" dealings, with the inevitable result that hedging and forward trading (other than purely physical) virtually ceased. In December 1916 complete Government control was instituted and all trading in copper, lead and zinc suspended. What at its outset had been assumed to be a brief war was now proving almost totally disruptive as it dragged on. The effect was to eliminate from the international scene more than half of the zinc smelting capacity which had been so heavily concentrated in Germany, Belgium and France.

This situation was the cause of a major shift in the balance of zinc production; the American smelting capacity was all but doubled by 1917, and for the first time the USA exported metal both to Britain and to France. In the previous year the UK Government had contracted to buy the bulk of the Australian ore over a 10-year period. Up till then, this had been going chiefly to the German smelters for refining and with the closure of this outlet the stocks had been building up in Australia since the outbreak of war. British smelting capacity started to expand as a result, and the foundations of Australia's own electrolytic smelting industry were laid with the establishment of a plant in Tasmania.

The position with lead, though less acute, was a roughly parallel one. German control of the Spanish mines was diluted and her own very large smelting industry deprived at the same time of much of its imported ore. Again, United States capacity was increased to fill the partial vacuum left by this situation and by the fact that Mexican

75

production had been brought to a standstill by a revolution in that country. However, the greatest expansion of lead smelting capacity took place in Australia whilst Canadian production was also stepped-up. Both these countries remained as producers of refined lead on a world scale. The war thus both demonstrated the extent of the German control over lead and zinc production and at the same time largely dissipated that control. At the centre of the network which owned, controlled or were virtually the only buyers of ores and concentrates in widely scattered areas stood Metallgesellschaft. Along with various banking interests this company was also a co-owner of Henry R. Merton in London which in turn controlled the Merton Metallurgical Company. Merton Metallurgical had a smelting plant in South Wales as well as interests in the USA and Australia. As the sole selling agent for these and other members of the Lead Association Metallgesellschaft was thus in control of a large part of the world output of lead up to the First World War.

The organisation – disrespectfully styled "the Octopus" – found itself progressively sundered as the war went on. Overseas subsidiaries for example were re-formed so as to retain control within their countries of domicile. After the armistice the United Kingdom Government was faced with the need to reorganise the 10-year purchasing agreement with the Australian producers on a commercial basis. For this reason, the British Metal Corporation was established in November 1918 with backing from London and from Australia. This corporation's role was expanded from its original one as a purchaser of Australian zinc to that of a developer of metal production throughout the Empire.

By its very existence, BMC did cause a measure of anxiety amongst the traders in London, and fears were expressed of a monopolistic distortion of the established pattern of marketing there: either by curbing the ability of the "independents" to buy from overseas, or by direct dealings producer to consumer. In the event these fears proved quite groundless. BMC has in fact been a Ring member of the LME for very many years, although its original nomenclature has been lost in mergers and re-organisations over the passage of time. (Sir Cecil Budd was Chairman of the Board of the Metal Market & Exchange Company at the same time as he served as first Chairman of the new BMC.)

The lead and zinc markets between the wars.
One curious effect of the transformation wrought on the lead and

zinc markets by the war was that, for the first time, dealings in these metals took place in the main Ring in January 1920. The hegemony which had existed pre-war had been swept away, and trading on the open market now took on a significance which it had not hitherto possessed – and this no doubt to the benefit of all, including those who had previously controlled a rather stultified market.

At first, prices of all metals fell in sympathy with declining armament orders; however it was not long before something of a boom occurred, with buying orders taking prices to historic high points. In February 1920 lead reached a price of £52 7s 6d and zinc £62 10s 0d; but reaction swiftly set in and in a year's time the prices had relapsed to £25 5s 0d and £23 10s 0d respectively. This reaction was the symptom of an overall recession in trade, which caused a situation of over-supply in all markets and notably in lead and zinc. In addition, the economic climate took a marked turn for the worse: a situation which began with the collapse of the Mark, and did not really end until after the Great Depression of 1929 to 1931. Demand in certain quarters – notably in the stripling automobile industry – did, however, give rise to some pressure on supplies. Improved methods of extraction of zinc from lead-zinc ores and increasing supplies of recycled lead (much of it recovered from old car batteries) in their turn increased the supply of these metals with the result that the general trend of prices continued downwards.

The decline in all prices began to be noticeable in the mid 1920s. One effect of the war had been greatly to increase productive capacity: with the coming on stream of modern and comparatively low-cost operations set up in Australia, Canada and elsewhere. Meantime the older-established European industry had perforce to continue to rely on less up-to-date plant, and to pay more for imported ores. Some sort of collective initiative by the European producers was felt necessary; perhaps with happy memories of the short-lived yet apparently successful Spelter Convention before the war, they formed the Zinc Cartel in May 1928.

At first the cartel was not an unqualified success. It was not until January of the following year that any form of agreement was reached as to policy; and even this agreement was far from wholehearted. There were some very basic differences in outlook between the members. Belgium and Poland, who were mainly concerned with exports, pressed for production controls whilst with an eye to their largely domestic markets Britain, France and Germany preferred some form of protective measures. The cartel also failed to attract the new (and expanding) producers of electrolytic zinc which had been set up, outside the traditional refining areas, in Australia, Canada and Mexico. These producers maintained the level of their exports to Europe and – electro zinc being of higher and a more consistent standard – made appreciable inroads on the market there. Prices, therefore, continued their downward trend and the cartel was abandoned at the end of 1929. There was talk of its revival, but no positive steps were taken. In 1931 the zinc price in London fell to an obviously uneconomic level – as low as £9 13s 9d – and it became clear to the producers that a further major co-operative effort on their part was essential if they were to protect their margins at all.

The International Zinc Cartel, formed in July 1931, was the outcome: this time all the main producers outside the USA became members. An overall reduction of output to 55% of agreed capacity was almost immediately accepted and implemented. By this means, production for the rest of the year, and 1932, was so reduced as to fall below world consumption, stocks declined correspondingly and prices took an upward turn at last.

Unfortunately for those concerned, other and very powerful disruptive influences made real co-operation between members of the cartel difficult if not actually impossible. Britain (the largest zinc importer) left the Gold Standard in September 1931. The ensuing depreciation of sterling and those currencies (*e.g*, the Australian pound) which moved with sterling brought a rise in the London (sterling) price which was greatly to their benefit, at the expense of producers whose currencies remained on gold. These countries were compelled to adopt protective measures in order to maintain their foreign exchange positions in the face of declining exports: amongst them were Belgium, France, Germany and Holland. To complete what was by now almost a scene of financial anarchy (with moratoria on most war debt payments already declared) the United States herself went off the Gold Standard in April 1933.

Tariffs and quotas.
It is small wonder, therefore, that in this climate, even traditionally free-trading countries such as the United Kingdom should have been led to seek protection for their own interests. The *Import Duties Act* was passed in 1932. This put an end to completely free trading with the imposition of import duties on a selective basis. At the same time the Ottawa Conference (1932) instituted the system of "Empire Preference" which was to last, as far as lead and zinc duties were

concerned, right up to the British accession to the Treaty of Rome. Other colonial powers took roughly comparable steps in their own interest: these taking the form of import restrictions or (in the case of Germany) export subsidies. The Ottawa Conference led the British Government to impose a duty of 10% *ad valorem* on all imports of zinc other than from Empire sources. By 1933 Australia, Canada and Rhodesia between them contributed some 80% of British imports, compared with 34% in 1930. Imports from these sources would have been greater still, had it not been for the quota restrictions imposed by the cartel, which was still in being. In 1933 the Germans introduced a system of premiums to domestic producers. These various unilateral steps by some of its members naturally strained the cartel, and there were demands for a revision of the quotas which had been observed only somewhat approximately in any case by the low-cost producers. This brought about the suspension of the cartel in January 1933, though it was renewed in March with what were hoped to be more compelling provisions for observation of the quota limits. These were increased over the ensuing two years as world consumption recovered, but the attraction of national rather than co-operative market protection proved too strong: the cartel being finally dissolved at the end of 1934.

The Lead Producers' Reporting Association was founded in April 1931 by the majority of the non-American producers. The reasons behind the formation of the association were similar to those which had brought the zinc cartels into being. Lead had been in over-production effectively since 1925, and stocks of surplus material had amassed to an alarming degree. The London price declined inexorably until at the end of 1930 it had reached a low of £14 12s 6d per ton. The association sought to remedy the situation by restrictions on output as well as by financing stocks. For a time the price was indeed steadied, but the devaluation of sterling after Britain went off the Gold Standard in 1931, and the imposition import duties by Britain the following year proved too much for the association to deal with and it was dissolved in March 1932. Prices fell once more (to £9 3s 9d in June 1932), although lead from Empire sources was attracted to London even at these levels. Meanwhile Belgium and Germany took action to protect their home industries, leaving the USA, Spain and Mexico to bear the worst effects of the depression. Producers in these latter countries were quick to seize on any apparent stimulation of consumer demand and to flood a not too receptive market with their own output. In 1934 silver prices rose, leading to a further increase in lead output in order to extract the now more valuable silver content. As with other strategic commodities it was not in fact until international tension began to mount – especially on the Italian "adventure" in Abyssinia – that demand began really to recover. In fact, by March 1937 the London price of lead had strengthened to £36 7s 6d, although this price was not sustained and there was a falling-off in the months following.

The Lead Producer's Association was brought into being in September 1938, having this time strong support from all leading producers outside the USA and Europe. The association worked on the basis of production limitations linked with price movements on the LME and changes in the tonnage in stocks. Thus restrictions initially were to be imposed if stocks rose to 150,000 tons or more, or the LME price fell below £15 0s 0d. Like the pre-war cartels, this association did little (or was required to do little) before its dissolution on the outbreak of the Second World War.

The LME contracts between the wars.
Both the Good Soft Pig Lead and Virgin Spelter contracts survived unaltered for many years after their introduction. This comparative longevity was not however achieved without a great deal of discussion and intermittent disagreement. The conflicting requirements of a contract broad enough in scope both to satisfy producers and to serve as a useful medium for hedging, and those of consumers who would have preferred something far more precise were always apparent. To these had to be added the complications as to shipping practices (and timetables) to which the lead and zinc contracts were particularly subject. In 1923 (20 years after introduction of the lead contract) there were strong arguments in favour of admitting Liverpool as an additional delivery point to London. Canadian and Mexican metal usually came to the United Kingdom via Liverpool and it was urged that registration of that port would facilitate the delivery of this metal on to the market. The Committee, however, felt otherwise, bearing in mind that London was then handling more than 70% of imported lead, and seeking also not to upset the important European trade which naturally made use of London rather than Liverpool. (In point of fact, London remained the only delivery point for LME lead until 1932.) The Virgin Spelter contract was amended to admit deliveries FOR Avonmouth in 1930: this in order

1 Whittington Avenue: the entrance to the London Metal Exchange is on the right, Leadenhall Market is in the background.

2 The entrance to the Exchange.

London Metal Exchange Company Lim.

At a Meeting of the Committee held at the Lombard Rooms. on Tuesday the 19th. day of December 1876 at 11. a.m.

Present.

Arthur Bird Esqr in the Chair
G.J. Von Dadelszen Esq.   W. Bentz Esq.
P.W. Spence Esqr   A.R. James Esq
J.F. Schwann jur Esq   T.K. Weir Esq
William Smith Esq   F.W. Bond Esq
C.G. Grenfell Esq   W. Sargant Esq

In Attendance.
Mr. Paine -

Resolved   That each Member of the Committee in Alphabetical order be Chairman in rotation for One Calender Month Mr. Bird to be the first Chairman and to hold Office till the 1st of February 1877, and under this Resolution the Chair was accordingly taken by Mr. Bird.

Resolved   That Messrs Barnett, Hoares, Hanbury & Lloyd be the Bankers of the Company and that an account be opened with them, Cheques to be signed by 2 Directors, and countersigned by the Secretary

3   The minutes of the first meeting of the Committee of the London Metal Exchange Company Limited, 19 December 1876.

At a meeting of the Committee
of Subscribers of the London Metal
Exchange, held at No 4 Lombard
Court on Thursday the 31st March
1881 at 12.45 pm

Present.
Mr Arthur Bird in the Chair
Messrs J S Campbell   A R James
K A James   G Richardson
W Sargant   J F Schwann Jr
J A Sargant   Wm Smith
A H Strauss   S W Spence
C C Turnbull   J R Weir
G S Von Dadelogen   R Bendy.

It was Proposed by Mr K H James
Seconded Mr J A Sargant &
Resolved That the Chairman & Deputy Chairman
be appointed in alphabetical order
for a fortnight, and failing the presence
of either at any meeting during
their time of office; the next in
rotation present to take their places

It was Proposed by Mr Bendy
Seconded by Mr Campbell and
Resolved That the tone of the Market be described
in as few words as possible.

It was Proposed by Mr Schwann
Seconded. Mr Von Dadelogen &
Resolved That the Report be issued at the same
time as hitherto and 3 to be a quorum.

4   The minutes of the first meeting of the Committee of Subscribers—
elected March 1881.

5 The bell now struck to mark the end of the kerb market each day. It dates from the completion of the present rooms in 1882.

6 The Ring during copper trading, *circa* 1950.

The London Metal Exchange.

With a view to carry out the expressed wishes of a large number of the Subscribers, it has been determined to form a new Company for taking over the present Metal Exchange, and to offer to all Subscribers the opportunity of taking an interest therein.

For this purpose a Company is in course of formation, and will shortly be registered, with a Capital of £10,000, in 500 Shares of £20 each, of which one-half will be payable on allotment, and no further call is contemplated.

The results of the working of the present Company have shown a satisfactory return on the Capital subscribed.

The new Company will be called " The Metal Exchange Company, Limited."

These arrangements having been come to by an understanding between the two Committees (Proprietors and Subscribers), it is hoped that every member of the Room will become a Shareholder.

The need of a larger Exchange has long been felt, and an opportunity now presents itself to obtain suitable premises on a plot of ground bounded on two sides by Leadenhall Street and Gracechurch Street, and for the acquisition of which, on lease, negotiations are now in progress. The rent is £1650 per annum, and the plans of the new building—which it is hoped will be completed in the course of next winter—can be seen here

A holding of not less than five Shares will be necessary as a qualification for Directorship, but no Shareholder will have more than one vote.

The Articles of Association provide that the Shares shall be held by Subscribers only, and the right of dealing with them will be restricted accordingly.

The first Directors will be the members subscribing to the Articles of Association of the new Company, namely, Messrs. J. P. Campbell, A. R. James, K. H. James, G. Richardson, P. W. Spence, A. Strauss, and R. Zunz, who will only hold office until the first General Meeting of the Company, which will take place within six months from date of registration, when the election of the Board will rest with the Shareholders.

The Directors will reserve full discretion as to the allotment of the Shares, but it may be mentioned that, although certain members have expressed their willingness to take up the whole of the Capital of the Company, it has been considered more desirable that the area of subscription should be as wide as possible, and an allotment will be made on that basis. Members wishing to take an interest will please fill up the annexed Form, and return this paper to the Secretary (Mr. Harradine) by the 16th instant.

4, LOMBARD COURT, E.C.,
9th July, 1881.

The Memorandum and Articles of Association may be seen at the Offices of the Solicitors of the Company, Messrs. Paines & Co., Gresham House.

THE LONDON METAL EXCHANGE.

I desire to take_____Shares, or any less number that may be allotted to me, in the new Company referred to in the the above Memorandum as now in course of formation, and which it is intended to register as "THE METAL EXCHANGE COMPANY, LIMITED"; and I agree to accept the Shares so alloted to me (upon which I shall be prepared to pay £10 per Share on allotment), and to become a member of the said Company. Failing my acceptance of the Shares or payment of the £10 per Share within fourteen days of allotment, the Directors will be at liberty to deal with them as they think fit.

(Signature)_____ Subscriber

Full Name _____

Address _____

Dated_____July, 1881.

To
MR. EDWARD HARRADINE,
The London Metal Exchange,
Lombard Court, E.C.

7 Prospectus of the Company as we now know it. Note that the Committee of Subscribers has already been formed.

MR. ALFRED M. BAER
ESSRS. HENRY GARDNER & CO. LTD.

MR. E. W. MORRICE
(MESSRS. HENRY BATH & SON, LTD.)

MR. G. S. SMITH
MESSRS. G. SMITH & SONS.

MR. CARL RICARD SEATED
MR. W. GARTSEN (ALSO Mr. KNIGHT)
(MESSRS. RICARD & FREIWALD.)

8 These caricatures were published originally in *Metal Bulletin* in the early 1930s, and subsequently in *Metal Bulletin Monthly* in October 1974. They are reproduced with the permission of the publishers © Metal Bulletin Ltd. 1976. Of those depicted the names of Smith and Morrice are amongst those still associated with the LME, whilst Messrs Ricard and Freiwald are referred to in Chapter 5.

9 A fish-eye view of the Room today.

The
London Metal Exchange
viewed by
continental eyes

12 & 13   "I'll take a hundred!"

14 "Eight bid."

15 A typical members' telephone booth.

16 Relaying information from Room to office and vice versa.

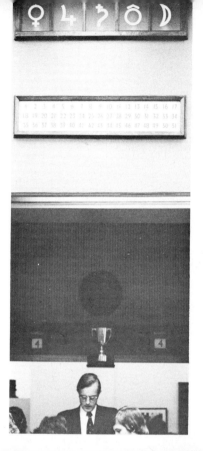

17 The Assistant Secretary of the Metal Market & Exchange Company reads the prices.

18 A Ring member's card in which his dealings are plotted.

19   A study in concentration.

20   "It is the responsibility of the seller to check all dealings."

21 Some tactical planning.

22 A trade is done—and recorded. There is no room for error.

23 "All dealings must be clearly audible to the Ring as a whole . .

24 LME Official warehouse, Rotterdam (Courtesy of C. Steinweg).

to accommodate the needs of the UK zinc smelting industry, itself largely a creation of the war years.

In terms of standardisation of metal deliverable against either contract there had been nothing at all laid down. Lead deliveries were reasonably consistent and complaints from consumers were few. Zinc was a different matter however, especially since the evolution of the distillation process. Complaints were heard quite frequently and the Committee's first reaction was to exhort producers to endeavour to maintain a higher and less variable standard. However, the zinc contract was losing ground due to the increased production of electrolytic zinc assaying 99.9 % and better. In common with lead, the zinc contract as it then stood laid down no terms as to deliverable brands or purity but was based upon ex-Government stocks with which the market had been re-started at the end of the First World War: and there were good ordinary brands assaying 98 % Zn. As the higher grades were at the time always in a position to command a premium over good ordinary brands (this was not always to be the case), they tended to be traded outside the LME contracts.

A further, and in a sense even knottier problem was possibly the introduction of the import duties in 1932. The duties were at the outset opposed by the LME on the two grounds that they would penalise British consumers, and that they would be detrimental to the Exchange's position as arbiter of world prices and as the world's ultimate "physical market of last resort". (Indeed, the latter was the prime reason for the maintenance of a duty-free world price at all.) The contracts were re-worded to include "United Kingdom import duty (if any) to be for buyer's account", and provision was made for a claw-back of duty in the event that foreign material was re-exported and not consumed within the United Kingdom. The trouble here was that metal imported from Empire sources came rapidly to command a premium equivalent to the duty imposed on foreign imports, were it sold privately outside the market. Consequently, this material practically disappeared from market trading, turnover fell accordingly, and LME prices came to be based to an excessive extent on dealings in foreign material which all too often was only offered there *faut de mieux*.

The situation was thus unhealthy for the market and for producers alike: the one saw turnover diminishing and the other saw prices (often needlessly low) based more and more on sales of production other than their own. The Committee of the LME and the Import Duties Advisory Committee of the UK Government held discussions

81

in August 1935. As a consequence, specific duties were imposed in lieu of the controversial *ad valorem* duties: amounting to a flat 7s 6d per ton on lead and 12s 6d on zinc imported from other than Empire sources. The LME contracts were also amended, to permit the seller either to deliver foreign metal at contract price with duty added, or domestic or Empire metal with an added premium equal to the amount of the duty. In either case the impost was for the buyer's account.

In this way, both Empire and foreign lead and zinc were traded in the Market on precisely the same basis as to price. What is equally important was that the impossibility of hedging an *ad valorem* duty on an as yet unknown price was also resolved. (As an historical note – the duty on zinc was raised to 30s per ton in 1939.)

The Second World War.
The outbreak of the Second World War once again saw all dealings on the LME in copper, lead and zinc suspended. Private stocks in the UK were requisitioned, and the new Ministry of Supply fixed maximum official prices for each. It was unfortunate that the Committee of the Exchange were not consulted beforehand, for these arbitrary prices were well below current market prices. (It is arguable that these latter may at the time have been a little over-high, in the light of immediately pre-war market sentiment.) Be that as it may, the closing out of open positions was not achieved without difficulty and even a measure of acrimony. The Ministry was also – to market eyes at least – dilatory in releasing metal for completion of delivery contracts, no doubt on account of a natural disinclination to part with strategic materials. In the event, lead and zinc deliveries were not completed until the end of February 1940.

The LME thus passed into a kind of limbo (tin dealings were suspended, and the Ring ceased to trade, on 8 December 1941 after the Japanese entry into the conflict threatened supplies from the East), and was to remain thus until 1944. Not that Board or Committee were idle: Rules were revised and a good deal of useful propaganda work undertaken. In 1944 discussions with the authorities were initiated with a view to a recommencement of free trading. Lead and zinc at this time were actually in surplus along with copper: only tin being scarce.

In May 1945 the UK Government terminated its long-term contracts with producers of lead and zinc, licences for domestic consumption became more readily available and imports actually reduced for a time as accumulated stocks were pressed into service. Government policy was still undecided however, and was no doubt rendered doubly cautious in the light of the serious disruption of, and actual damage to, sources of supply which the war had occasioned. In point of fact it was not for some three or four years after the cessation of hostilities that supply positions could be regarded as in any way restored.

However, the demand situation was causing concern; the United States appeared as a consumer of heroic proportions (60% of the free world's copper and 40% or so of lead and zinc), and in consequence emerged for the first time as an importer. Coupled with the desire on the part of most other countries to acquire US dollars, this new trend put a considerable impetus into rising prices for all metals.

As an indication of price movements, lead had been pegged at £25 per ton throughout the war. It rose to £55 by July 1946 and to £90 by May 1947. The bulk-buying policy of the Government was too inflexible, the Ministry's requirements too large for them to be other than a focus of attention whenever it came into the world market. Worse still, when the inevitable downward trend started in early 1949 the Ministry lowered its own selling prices to UK consumers far too cautiously and clumsily. The outcome was that in May of that year the London price of zinc was £24 per ton dearer than in New York – and the lead price £18 dearer.

For a brief period, the Ministry attempted to follow New York prices, and a very limited form of hedging was permitted to British consumers in that they could book forward orders (on payment of a premium) as a form of cover against rising prices. There was no comparable cover for merchants or holders of stocks against falls in prices however. This well-intentioned half measure on the one hand, and a real concern as to use of metals in "commodity shunting" operations involving further exchange losses were enough to stay the Government's hand until the re-opening of the tin market – tin being a sterling commodity – in November 1949.

Conditions generally became far less easy after that date, and it is of interest to note that – still controlled and dealt with entirely by the Ministry of Materials, as it was now styled – prices for lead rose to £180 per ton and zinc to £190 in August 1951. Even higher prices were obtaining on the black market: £140 for zinc and £200 for lead at the time. The Ministry was once again caught with long-term buying orders at high prices when the market declined once more after the end of the Korean war. Once again recourse was made to following

New York prices, but despite fairly savage cuts (£60 per ton in May and June 1952) the London prices remained uneconomically high in relation to those in New York and on the Continent.

The markets re-opened.
Clearly the situation could not be allowed to continue. After further hesitation the Government (now a Conservative one) announced that dealings in lead would be freed as from 1 October 1952. At the same time, Government purchasing and the issue of licences were done away with, and the Bank of England scheme (initiated with the re-opening of dealings in tin) was extended to cover the foreign exchange aspect of lead dealings. Cash lead was made available, and the Ministry was also a lender of lead – through the "Government Broker" – until private supplies were restored.

Resumption in dealings brought at first a heavy fall in prices. The Ministry's last selling price had been £131 per ton; this was known to be unrealistic since it was still based on the New York price, which was derived from a very narrow and somewhat isolated market. The European "going price" was £95. In the event the LME price after three weeks of free trading stood at £80. There was soon a recovery as consumers started seriously to buy, yet the producers at the time were not very pleased with the immediate outcome of the return to free trading after some years of insulation from market forces.

The zinc market on the LME was re-opened on 2 January 1953. There had been a little more caution in this case, as it had to be taken into account that some 50% of UK imports of zinc came at the time from Canada and the USA. A drain in dollar reserves could therefore have ensued. As against this, experience with tin and lead had shown that a fall in prices was to be expected – so reducing the strain on the country's exchange position. The latter forecast proved correct, with prices rapidly falling from the Ministry's £110 right down to £63 10s 0d by the end of April.

With the freeing of dealings in copper on 5 August 1953 the LME was once more fully operational – after an eclipse lasting 14 years.

At this point, it is only right to mention the name of Mr J. D. ("Jimmy") Wolff, who came to the market as an Authorised Clerk in 1904, chaired the Committee for a remarkable span from 1928 until 1950 save for one year, and the Board from 1946 to 1961. He was largely responsible for all the re-negotiations with Ministers during the war years and those immediately following, in which he was well supported by P. W. Smith, the uncle of the redoubtable

84

Philip Smith, who is the present Chairman of the Board. Smith and Wolff are names which can trace an uninterrupted connexion with the Exchange from its foundation to the present time, and the combination of P. G. Smith and Fred Wolff still hold the Chairs of Board and Committee respectively.

A world surplus of lead developed during the 1950s. In consequence of this, and of the imposition of protective measures by some of the producing countries (in December 1957 the LME price had sunk to £70), the United Nations set up the Lead and Zinc Conference in 1959. Prices continued to fall: lead being at £61 17s 6d in December 1960, and a year later falling to £57 12s 6d. The conference was developed into the Lead-Zinc Study Group and whose members meet each year at a conference in Geneva.

The lead price did show a recovery as far as £154 10s 0d late in 1964, but fell away once more as over-supply combined with concern as to lead pollutant effects (especially as an additive in motor fuel) down to a low of £84 in late 1972. There was a recovery in the boom of 1973 to 1974, whereafter the price again fell away, despite the efforts of producers to support it by buying on the LME.

Zinc prices were sustained in the 1950s by growing demand, and by stockpiling in the USA, to peak at £96 17s 6d in December 1959. After two years of uncertainty, during which a low of £62 was recorded in August 1962, zinc prices advanced once more to reach £148 10s 0d in July 1964. This rapid advance brought a measure of concern as to substitution (plastics for galvanised products, for example), and on 13 July 1964 the Imperial Smelting Company issued a statement to the effect that, as stocks of zinc in LME warehouses were reduced to a "negligible tonnage" the producers supplying the UK and Continental markets considered LME prices no longer realistic. The Imperial Smelting Company therefore decided to give the lead by introducing their own price of £125 per ton. "This price" the statement read, "is effective today and will remain in force until further notice."

The LME price fell shortly afterwards, and the Imperial Smelting Company's – or European producer – price was lowered to £110. In May the following year the LME price dipped below the European producer price again, and the producers revised their prices downwards to £102 and in June 1967 to £98. This was then raised once more to £114 6s 8d after Britain's devaluation in November. Thereafter the LME price and the producer price moved in a narrow band: usually in sympathy, usually with the LME standing at a discount roughly equal to the cost of duty and shipment from the Continent to the United Kingdom. The European zinc producers' system makes use of a "fixed" price which varies from time to time on the more frequent variations in the LME price. At the same time, the producers can and do move to support LME prices by themselves operating on the market. The success or otherwise of the systems is somewhat clouded by the fact that the LME contract remains 98% Zn (good ordinary brand) whilst much of the material in use is of higher purity with consequential premiums over the LME prices. There have been times, however, when the market has been further confused by shortages of good ordinary brand – whose lead content makes it a requirement of the galvanising trade – and surplus of high grade or special high grade. Perhaps things will not really be satisfactory until the LME introduces a high grade zinc contract as has already been done in the case of tin.

The lead and zinc contracts after the Second World War.
The original GSR lead and Virgin Spelter contracts enjoyed a remarkably long span of life. It was not until after the war that changes were made which brought them more on a par with the current contracts for copper and tin. On the reopening of the Exchange for dealings in lead and zinc, the contracts were changed in order to limit deliverable material to any one of a number of approved brands: a measure, this, of protection to the consumer.

It was not until July 1960 that, as with lead, the delivery terms in the zinc contract were amended from ex-ship to in-warehouse for prompts maturing after 1 October; the warehouse warrant thus became for these two metals also, the basic document traded in respect of LME dealings. (The changeover resulted in an immediate increase of about £1 in prices.) This alteration was only effected after much discussion between Board and Committee culminating in a General Meeting of subscribers held in March 1960. In 1966 Rotterdam was added to the delivery points for lead and zinc. This greatly altered the pattern of trading, since the Rotterdam warehouses were in a position to store metal without payment of duty or premium unless or until that material was taken into use within the European Economic Community or (if dutiable) within the United Kingdom. Further complications arose: to the extent that in later years stocks of Korean zinc in Rotterdam reached large proportions due to complications over import quotas of Eastern Bloc metal permitted to enter the Community. For a time it appeared as though the LME were destined to be a home for this "homeless" metal, until changing conditions in 1973–74 drastically reduced stocks and changed the whole picture. (The Committee had in fact approved Hamburg as a delivery point for lead and zinc in December 1973.) It is possible that further amendments may need to be made to the zinc contract, and a split into GOB and high grade is quite frequently canvassed. In its present form the contract admits delivery of GOB zinc assaying not less than 98% Zn. Higher grade brands may be, and are, traded at a premium against the contract but the main problem rests not so much on a matter of purity as of different end-use. It is less a matter of higher grade than of a "different animal" altogether. A further alteration to the contract was made in 1973, when the requirement that duty, if any, be for buyer's account, was deleted. This was done in anticipation of a proposed alteration of the basis of the Common External Tariff of the EEC on lead and zinc from a flat rate to an *ad valorem* basis. Omission of the "buyer's account" requirement would put the onus of paying the duty (or premium for domestic production) on to the ultimate purchaser for consumption. In the event that a change is made in due course to an *ad valorem* basis, dealings on the Exchange would therefore continue to be priced free of any such duty and the LME prices thus kept truly international.

To sum up the development of the lead and zinc contracts it would only be fair to say that they are in some ways less satisfactory than those in the other metals. In part this is due to the quality requirements in the contracts themselves (though less so in the case of lead), and the scope these requirements allow for impurities. In this context, it is not so much a matter of a percentage of impurity, as of the nature of whatever other material may be present. In the case of zinc, a high lead content makes a particular brand unsuitable for some purposes though quite acceptable for others, and the system of brand identification unfortunately is not such as to enable a consumer to know instantly how metal on warrant, and which he may have taken up, is composed. On the other hand, as they are set out, the contracts do provide a sufficiently wide base as to be eminently practicable as hedging and pricing media. It is therefore not quite such a simple matter as might at first appear: since one fairly general contract may undoubtedly be better from this important standpoint than two more restrictive ones.

In the lead and zinc contracts therefore – and especially in the case of the latter – this incompatibility between the hedging and the physical requirements is at its most apparent.

7

The Silver Market on the LME

As a means of exchange, silver has a longer history, at least in Europe, than gold. The fact that until very recent times silver was in wide use as a constituent of coinage still exercises a measure of influence over the market in the metal; its use as an investment medium is as important in market terms as its manifold uses in industry and electronics as well as more traditionally in jewellery and the decorative trade.

Today's silver market on the LME is in fact the third market there in this metal. The first was instituted as early in the Exchange's history as 1897, when dealings in silver were admitted for the first time to the main Ring. Such a development became feasible when the bullion merchants took the step of issuing warrants in respect of metal held by them in store. This first LME silver market endured until the start of the First World War, though it had in actual fact been virtually moribund since about 1911.

The second silver market commenced operations in 1935, but once again interest waned, and the market ceased to operate at the outbreak of war in 1939. It was not reopened after the cessation of hostilities, although the subject was discussed, and no further developments took place until the 1960s.

The London Silver Market here commands attention, since it has been in existence – commencing with a weekly price fixing – since the 1880s. Daily trading took place between these regular fixings, and at about the beginning of this century daily fixings were instituted: for both spot and forward prices. In its earlier years the market had always been to some extent haunted by the spectre of monetary silver. Though this direct connexion between the metal and currencies has been eroded to the point of disappearance, silver remains today a very important medium for hedging currency values. The activities of the young LSM were, however, for the most part in the role of an *entrepôt* market, between producers in the Americas and buyers located chiefly in China and India. Its dealings, however, were always subject to the vagaries of government decisions and to changes in monetary policy: at that time the metal still had a direct and important part to play in such matters.

The first changes in this pattern of trade occurred with the advent in 1933 of President Roosevelt's New Deal Administration in the USA. American silver prices were raised, with a consequent reversal of the flow of demand – this time from Asia back to the United States – to the extent of forcing China to abandon the Silver Standard. After some 18 months thus, the American Administration altered its policy to one of purchasing only domestically produced silver. A special Silver Profits Tax was also imposed on US dealers, and for the duration of this tax silver ceased to be traded on the New York Commodity Exchange. In this way, the US Treasury was able to amass very large quantities of silver into its coffers.

After the Second World War, the growth of the electronics industry added a new dimension to the demand for silver (already widely used in X-ray and photographic emulsions as well as in more traditional decorative guises), and in consequence demand began greatly to outstrip supply: even though the latter was from time to time augmented by releases from privately hoarded stocks. The balance of the American official stocks was released from time to time by the US Treasury at a fixed price: until in 1961 "free stocks" in the USA were exhausted. London prices – dominated by the New York price – had varied between 77*d* and 80*d* per ounce: equivalent to 89 to 92 cents. The US official selling price was raised in 1963 to 129.3 cents per ounce.

This was in fact the highest to which the price could have been raised, without the silver content of the then US coinage actually exceeding the face value of that coinage. This had the effect of putting some sort of ceiling over prices in London too, and they remained approximately constant at around 112*d* until 18 May 1967: when US sales to foreign buyers were terminated. This move signalled an instant leap by the London price of 18½*d* to 130*d* per ounce: the largest increase since the 1949 sterling devaluation.

On 14 July 1967 the USA abandoned its attempts at maintaining a ceiling on silver prices, and sales were limited to two million ounces per week, to American industrial users only. These from stocks which at the beginning of 1959 had totalled 1900 million ounces. (During the same period, the USA had abandoned silver coinage and gone over to the cupro-nickel "sandwich" coin.)

By late 1967 the American Treasury was further embarrassed by the decline in the stocks available to it of .999 fine bars which at the time were the accepted standard grade for the greater part of both domestic and overseas business. On 12 October that year, the US Treasury suspended sales of silver of this quality: offering instead bars of .996 and .998 fine. At the same time it was announced that these lower grades would only be delivered against "Silver Certificates", or one dollar bills first issued in 1878 and redeemable in silver. There were in fact 2127 million dollars worth of these bills in circulation at the close of 1960. In the following year any further issue was cancelled, and the old bills were called in. Nonetheless, there were many who chose to hold them, and in 1967 there were still some 375 million or more in circulation. The last day for redemption of these Silver Certificates was fixed at 24 June 1968.

The devaluation of sterling in November 1967 brought a peak in London silver prices, and on 14 December the market there reached its high of $224\frac{3}{4}d$ per ounce.

Silver once again on the LME.

It was hardly surprising that these developments had not been allowed to pass unnoticed by the LME. The question of re-instituting LME dealings in silver was raised in June 1967, after several members had expressed interest. Talks were held with the bullion brokers, who evinced surprise at the proposition mixed with a measure of disapprobation; but it was agreed that the discussions should be continued.

In the meantime, both the Bank of England and the Board of Trade were consulted and neither objected. The LME Committee therefore set up a sub-committee in order to go into the matter in detail, and to draw up a contract. It soon became plain to all that this contract would have to be somewhat different from those currently in force for the other metals: notably as to the duration of the permitted forward trading period. Something longer than three months but not longer than 13 was the general consensus: but opinions varied as to precisely how long the period should be. Eventually, the sub-committee came down in favour of a seven months period. It was felt that this would attract business from the USA and from the Continent as well as from within the United Kingdom.

The Silver Contract has a definite place in the history of the LME documents, in that for the first time ever, the margin to be called from the client by the member in the event of a price movement adverse to the former was put on a mandatory as distinct from a discretionary basis. This was felt to be necessary in view of the relatively greater length of the contract and consequentially larger scope for such price movements during its course. (An argument against longer-term contracts in the other metals is that margins might then need to be mandatory, with the possibility of disturbing cash-flow considerations in hedging by industry.) Thus, a margin of 10% was laid down from the outset as essential on opening a silver contract. This could be made up by cash or a bank guarantee, and was to be maintained at 10% of the value of the contract throughout its life. Calls were to be made in steps, whenever the price difference exceeded 50% of the original margin. However, like all the LME contracts, the silver contract was set up as an agreement between principals. A side-effect of this running true to tradition was that the margin was (and is) called by the LME member himself and not via any sort of clearing house.

Contractual lots were fixed at 10,000 troy ounces of silver assaying not less than .999 fine; and there was some discussion as to whether these lots might be made up of mixed brands or not. Originally, storage of silver on warrant was in vaults in the Westminster Bank in London and the AmRo Bank in Amsterdam; later, storage by the Commerzbank in Hamburg was added.

Dealings commence.

In February 1968 the new silver contract was launched on the LME. At the outset, the contract confounded the sceptics (who saw little future for two parallel silver markets in London) and the first year's turnover totalled 21,419 lots of 10,000 ounces. However, prices declined appreciably from an early peak in May of 264*d* to a low of 161*d* in June the following year: a fall of nearly 40% in direct contrast to the currently rising prices in the other metals.

It is likely that this early divergence by the silver market from the paths taken by those in the base metals arose out an of astute realisation by speculators of the virtues of the contracts as a currency hedge. Without the restrictions attached to trading in gold, and still retaining memories (if nothing more tangible) of its days as a monetary metal,

91

silver undoubtedly possesses great attraction in this context.

In the meantime, the US silver stocks had come down from 1900 million ounces in 1959 to 110 million only by 1970 – rather less than one quarter of annual world demand. At the time, demand world-wide was running well ahead of mine production, though the markets were "topped up" from time to time by releases from hoards as well as by a fairly consistent flow of secondary material. The sources of these replenishments were mainly India and Pakistan, in what was at the time an illicit trade via the Trucial States bordering the Persian Gulf, and from the remelting of demonetarised coin. This accumulation developed to such an extent that private holdings actually rose by nearly 220 million ounces: roughly equal to the year's sales by the US Treasury to consumers, for minting and in redemption of Silver Certificates. GSA Stockpile sales were to cease in 1970, by which time it was thought that supply and demand for industrial (excluding speculative) purposes would be approximately in balance. With the speculators – and currency hedging – as the big imponderables therefore, the LME silver market looked both highly uncertain as to prices and highly stimulating; already in early 1969 the prospects for a contract of longer duration than seven months were being canvassed. It was felt that a 12 or 13 months period would attract further business, especially from New York.

The sterling situation in 1969.
LME dealings in silver had been brought within the scope of the Bank of England Metals Scheme for foreign exchange from the inception of the contract. Members, therefore, were under the same disciplines as already applied to their trade with non-residents in the other metals.

Towards the end of 1969 the UK Treasury became concerned at the increasing stocks of silver in London, whose purchase from other than British residents was felt to be putting an undue strain on the country's reserves. In December the Bank of England obtained the agreement of the bullion brokers that they would reduce the level of their silver stocks financed by UK residents – where necessary – to the levels obtaining at the beginning of that year. The Bank also communicated with the LME and meetings took place between members of the Exchange's Bank of England Liaison Committee and representatives of the Bank, in order to arrive at a *modus operandi* whereunder any surplus should not "spill over" on to the LME and so reduce the effectiveness of the restraint accepted by the bullion brokers. (In fact, LME members who dealt in silver were to be asked by the Bank to agree to a "base level" of UK financed stocks and not to exceed that level. These base levels were to be set at figures obtaining later in the year than those accepted by the bullion brokers, and thus could be said to represent a lesser degree of restriction.)

It was also suggested that LME members might see fit or be able to finance their stocks by overseas borrowing or by "lending" silver to non-resident clients: even to the extent of using Euro-dollars for the purpose.

The Committee were greatly vexed by the element of compulsion embodied in these proposals and were not shy of voicing their feelings. However, agreement to co-operate with the request was not withheld, and through the Liaison Committee regular and close contact was maintained with the Bank. Resistance from the LME was naturally based on the two possibilities of the London market – and the London price – losing its authoritativeness, and even of other markets being set up as a result of London's temporary loss of freedom of action.

The Metals Scheme here came into its own. The LME had pointed out to the Bank that under the principal's contract the Exchange as such was not in a position to "police" its members' silver positions. In the event, these continued to be disclosed in confidence by participating members to the appropriate department of the Bank itself. The crisis gradually resolved itself and no coercive measures were in the end found necessary. Instead, the voluntary limitations agreed to by LME and London Silver Market members proved adequate.

A longer contract is proposed.

In June 1971 the Committee again turned its attention to the possibility of a silver contract with a longer forward dealing period than seven months. A sub-committee had been looking into the matter and had come forward with the suggestion that the period be extended to 13 months – this with an eye to more business from clients in the USA as well as arbitrage with Comex in New York. Another innovation was that the margin should henceforth be discretionary (as in the other contracts) as contrasted with mandatory.

The problem was that of security against price movements in a long-duration contract without enforced margins, and an extremely ingenious solution was proposed. In brief, this was based on the continuance of "traditional" daily dealings up to three months forward, with periodic settlements of differences on a monthly

93

basis thereafter. The settlement prices for these ensuing months would be worked out as the average of the three months sellers for the preceding five market days plus or minus the average of the difference between the three month and 13 month sellers for the same five days, divided *pr rata* for each month and rounded up to the nearest 0.1p (the minimum fluctuation in silver since decimalisation of the pound). It was of course intended that cash, three, seven and 13 months prices would be quoted each day. These settlements were to take place, as near as holidays permitted, on the fifteenth day of each month after the third month. This in order to ensure that every position beyond three months was subject to at least one such intermediate settlement, and that the only time when anyone could have more than one month's run before an intermediate settlement would be when his position had moved into the normal three months period.

Another point in favour of the proposed periodic settlements beyond three months, apart from that of security, was that such settlements provided only for 10 positions (dates). Were the traditional daily prompts system to have been projected so far forward, it would have produced a plethora of dates up to 13 months ahead – with consequent difficulty in quoting a meaningful price for each, in view of the uncertain volume of deals done on each of so many dates.

In sum, this was a most ingenious and worthy scheme, and one which if put into effect might well have served as a model for the oft-discussed lengthening of the contracts in the other metals. It was in fact discussed at length in the ensuing months (along with a possible delivery point for silver in New York), and it was put to the Board by the Committee in the spring of 1972. The Board came back with the suggestion that there be two contracts – one for thee months and another for longer periods – and at the end of April a letter was sent to all Ring members enclosing copies of the proposed contract, and asking for their views. A Meeting of Subscribers (a rare occurrence on the LME) was held on 8 June 1972, at which attendance was on the whole disappointing. However, it was taken that those in attendance were in the main in favour of adopting the new proposal, and it is quite possible that the matter might have been taken further on the strength of this meeting.

Earlier in that year however (in mid-March, to be exact), there had occurred the collapse of an LME Ring member company: albeit not as a result of LME dealings, but of an ill-advised effort to establish

94

a corner in a metal not traded and therefore un-hedgeable on the market. This sad affair somewhat dampened enthusiasm for anything like a contract with an even longer forward period than the existing seven months: at least until the Exchange had had time to take stock of its internal security arrangements, and the matter has not to date been revived.

The pound sterling floated.

There is a body of opinion which holds that the level at which the UK authorities had held the parity of sterling before it was floated in July 1972 was too high to be realistic. Correct or not as this view may be, the fact remains that the immediate result of the decision to free the pound to find its own level in the markets did at the outset bring about a somewhat abrupt devaluation. This alteration in parity was of course reflected in LME prices.

Silver responded to a greater degree than the other metals: prices rising by some 17% as compared with an average 5% for copper, lead and zinc. (The tin market thereupon became a more complicated affair, with the Buffer Stock Manager deciding to price in Malaysian dollars per picul rather than in pounds per tonne; effectively for the time the Penang price took the lead over London.)

The attractiveness of silver as a means of hedging or actually taking advantage of changes in relative currency parities has since then sustained LME dealings in silver at a respectably high level. Its future seems assured after this, the third essay at an LME market in the metal, and it is noteworthy that new brands of silver registered as good delivery on the market emanate from sources which are widely spread both geographically and ideologically. The relationship with the bullion brokers has developed smoothly to the point at which the two markets can be said to be truly complementary. What now remains to be seen is whether the protagonists of a longer contract come forward once more with a proposition which could, if successfully followed through, serve as a model for trading in the other metals as well.

PART THREE

8

Ring Dealing

The real kernel of the whole structure of the LME is the Ring. Notwithstanding the large turnover transacted each day by direct contact between members, and between members and clients, it is upon the comparatively brief Ring sessions that the whole pricing edifice of the LME is based. Though trading in the Ring by open outcry has a long history in the context of the LME, and despite its accepted status today as the true reflection of market sentiment, it was not ever thus. Indeed, in the early and formative years anything like the present marvellously concise Ring trading was just not possible. The developments which in the event made it possible should briefly be traced.

In the early years of the Exchange, trading was to all intents and purposes limited to spot dealings in metal actually available within the United Kingdom. Communications then were such that it was not yet a practical possibility to have any advance news of ship movements. However, in the 1840s the means were found for making it possible to be advised in advance of the arrivals of shiploads from the continent of Europe; later the same facility became available (via fast steam packet travelling more predictably than cargo vessels under sail) in respect of deliveries from the Straits and from South America. But it was the advent of the telegraph – as yet by ground line only and not yet truly wire-less – which transformed the whole picture as to information. By the mid 1870s there were cable links with virtually all the then major sources of raw material supply, and these links made possible the trade in materials for sale "on arrival of ship". This was the first significant step towards future trading as it is now universally understood.

Arrivals trading was of great benefit to merchant and consumer alike. It was now possible to strike a firm price for a future delivery, and therefore to have a measure of initiative as to when was the moment to strike that price. Once done, the trader could think ahead on the basis of an established price and rid himself of the bogey of adverse price movements before delivery of the material. The business was still a very mixed one though, and the wide variety of types and specifications of deliveries, as well as of arrival dates and delivery locations prevented any nearer approach to true terminal market trading. This extreme divergence between the various physical descriptions ruled out anything like the precise hedging which is today so much a part of market trading: based as it is on the "common denominator" of metal of a more or less universally acceptable specification and traded in standard weights in known locations.

The impetus, however, had been provided, and from arrivals trading – still truly a spot, or delivery market in a wide spectrum of grades and delivery points – the progress towards today's techniques was relatively rapid. Unfortunately, very little is documented as to how the various steps were made. What had to be evolved were the introduction of standard contract tonnages and grades, and the growth of dealing for dealing's own sake. Given a standard trading "lot" and given a counterparty to a contract who had his own reasons for trading as such, and the whole structure of hedging, pricing and market jobbing could be built up. As far as we know, it was between the 1870s and 1880s that these next fundamental moves were made which in turn made Ring dealing a practical possibility.

The "continuous market" emerges.
From the plethora of types and grades of materials traded, Chile bar copper and Straits tin – together with "foreign spelter", or zinc for the most part from German sources – began to emerge as the dominant grades in terms of tonnage traded. Simplicity of agreeing on terms for selling and buying a comparatively standard product itself generated more turnover; and further standardisation of the physical require-ments to be met by each parcel assisted the process. Delivery points were already becoming habitual, if not yet formalised into the present system of approved and registered warehouses. With the crystallisa-tion of the forward dealing period at three months – the average voyage time from port of embarkation to port of destination – and the

establishment of standard tonnages per parcel traded, the formative process was to all intents and purposes complete.

The one basic quality of a true terminal market – complete continuity – could now be brought into being as a reality. Generally accepted contract terms (though the truly standard LME contract document of today was still some way off), and trading lots of known weight and acceptable quality available at known delivery points, enabled market trading to begin to assume its present pattern of interlocking deals maturing on future dates in an unbroken thread. The tradition – unique to the LME amongst terminal markets – of trading in days rather than delivery months derives from its origin in arrivals on actual dates to which was grafted the concept of futures dealings for their own sake. The tradition remains valid in the light of the high proportion of physical business still traded on the LME; unlike the majority of other commodity markets which have in the course of time become futures markets almost to the exclusion of trading in actual deliveries.

The coming of the speculator.

In terms solely of taking risks – positions – on fluctuations in prices, there had been an element of speculation from the earliest days of arrivals dealings. A consumer of metals for fabrication into finished or semi-finished products was able to buy forward on arrival and thus know in advance the price to which he was committed. In the same way, a merchant who aimed to sell-on as soon as the goods were landed, might indulge in a little informed gambling by buying now "for arrival", and reckoning that in due time he could re-sell at a higher price to a customer. He could, if he wished, hold the material himself in anticipation of a better price rather than dispose of it immediately on arrival: when prices could very well be temporarily depressed due to a large tonnage being unloaded at one time.

From this – with its attendant costs of storing and financing metal held in the merchant's own stocks – there rapidly evolved the more attractive technique of buying for arrival, and then re-selling the (by now) standardised contracts to a purchaser without actually handling the metal himself at all. Indeed, it was more than likely still to be at sea. The concomitant technique of selling short in anticipation of falling prices was equally practicable. If he had forecast aright, the speculator could buy spot at a lower price and deliver this in liquidation of his forward sale.

The speculator became an established fact – and it was not long

101

before his usefulness also became recognised. His activities brought to the market a most necessary fluidity and effectively dampened any tendency by purely trade interests to create a one-way market. To this day, the same useful function is performed by those who come into the market for financial rather than (or as well as) trade reasons only. By sheer force of numbers, speculators can from time to time bring about an exaggeration of a market trend (especially in times of reduced trade activity), but even if they so wished they are never in a position to prolong such trends unduly. Only very rarely do speculators actually initiate a trend on the market – they follow rather than lead. In the first place, trade influence must in the event prove stronger; and secondly a market so thin as to allow speculation to spark-off a trend is both unusual and of very short duration. (During such a period, though, it is arguable that speculative activity generating some movement in an otherwise featureless market can only be for the good – granted that such initiative will soon be overtaken by trade dealings once more.)

The Ring.

Dealing in, or around the "Ring" chalked on the floor of the Exchange had been banned in 1881, but was reinstituted in April 1882 and has been continuous ever since – save only for market closure during the war years. At the reopening of trading in the Ring in 1882, dealing times were notably brief – from 11.50 a.m. to twelve noon and from 3.40 p.m. to 3.50 p.m. (To those, and they are not a few, who feel that today's Ring sessions from 12 noon to 1.05 p.m. and from 3.35 p.m. to 4.35 p.m. with attendant kerb dealing sessions are even now too short, these earlier times must appear to have been almost unworkable.) In point of fact they were very soon increased, and when for a time dealings in pig iron were also included, the practice arose of separating the dealings in each metal into individual 10-minute periods. Though iron has long since ceased to be traded on the LME, the separate "Rings" remain: now reorganised into two separate five-minute periods for each metal per Ring session.

In the 1890s the Secretary and his handbell made their début in the Ring. A clang of the bell and a cry of "Copper gentlemen, copper" commenced the day's proceedings; after the allotted time, checked by the Secretary's watch, a further ring of the bell and the next metal was announced. This tradition survived until the present system of electronic timing accompanied by the harsh clangour of an electric bell was introduced. Now, the Secretary's rostrum is used officially only for calling out the daily official prices and for the making of announcements. The system of levying fines for those careless enough to be overheard bidding or offering after the bell remains: on occasions when one of the doyens of the Ring is so caught out, there is a general and joyous cry of "Pay up!" from around the ring.

At first, lead and spelter (zinc) were traded separately from copper and tin in a smaller Ring of their own, and the metals were not all merged into the one until after the First World War. The possibility of reviving the practice of a second Ring in order to encourage trading in some of the "Minor Metals" (antimony, mercury, tungsten, etc.) is canvassed from time to time. It would appear to have its attractions if only because most of the LME Ring dealing firms maintain a department specialising in other than the four main base metals. Such an innovation – or revival of an earlier practice – could well lead to one or more of the minor metals eventually being traded in the main Ring as was the case with lead and zinc. These metals started their LME life in a subsidiary market for reasons of lack of standardisation of grades and contracts: precisely the argument now levelled against trading in the minor metals of today.

Kerb dealings.
Before embarking on a fuller description of trading in the Ring – its rationale and its techniques – the institution of kerb as well as pre-market or inter-office trading must be touched upon.

The restricted times allowed for official dealings led naturally to members remaining in the Room after the final bell and continuing to do business amongst themselves. Reasons for this were many and quite genuine. For example, a member might have an unusually large tonnage to trade and would wish to do so without letting it influence the official prices to his or his client's detriment. Accordingly, he would trade what he could in the Ring, and then endeavour to buy or dispose of the balance in member-to-member dealings afterwards.

The LME authorities took the view that too much kerb dealing might give the practice an undue importance, and even undermine the authoritativeness of the official prices: a quite tenable point of view. Accordingly, they made fairly continuous and determined endeavours to restrain unofficial dealings, but met with little success.

Closure of the Room sharp at the end of official trading merely led to a noisy market being conducted in the street outside (hence, quite simply, the name "kerb" market); finally the authorities bowed to the inevitable and set aside a limited period after each official Ring session for kerb trading.

The practice continues, though today members take their seats or deal from positions identifiable with them, rather than stand – as they used to within living memory – in a tight circle around the centre of the Ring. All metals are traded simultaneously during kerb sessions without the official bell or the coloured lights which signify each metal as it is traded in turn during official dealings. As a natural overflow or relief-valve after a particularly busy session, as well as a useful vehicle for making various purely book-squaring transactions, the kerb market performs a valuable function.

Pre-market or inter-office dealings.

These have a particular significance in that to a great extent they make up the process by which a large number of enquiries and orders – from the firmest down to the most tentative – may be pieced together into a logical pattern before Ring trading commences. The principal's contract makes it possible for a member to deal direct with his clients, and he may therefore quite properly "ring-off" matching buying and selling orders direct, without necessarily executing them in the Ring: unless of course the client has instructed that his order be so traded.

Fabricators, and other purchasers of physical metal who are taking advantage of Pricing Terms will also place their buying orders with the member of their choice before the day's official dealings begin. Once the pattern of the day's orders and prices begins to form by way of written, telexed or telephoned requests and instructions, members are in a position to organise their own market cards for the day's Ring trading. By direct communication one with another beforehand the process may be expedited, and in course of this quite a respectable turnover of actual business is done.

Because the LME has no clearing house, nor any centralised system of recording or registering all trades done, it is not easy to make an estimate of the proportion of each member's daily turnover which is transacted by way of pre-market dealings; but it is safe to say that it is a pretty considerable proportion. The Exchange works on a virtually round the clock basis, and with the facility of communication now available, time – in terms of what hour of the day it may happen to be in London, Sydney, Singapore or New York – matters very little. There has to be a moment in each day when that day's prices are announced, and there has to be an adequate period of public bidding and offering to form a base for those prices. To trade in the Ring from the start of a working day in London would not necessarily produce a more (or a less) relevant price to a client the other side of the world. And for practical purposes such a prolonged Ring session would be both difficult to organise and extremely wasteful of effort: in that much of it would inevitably be taken up with establishing the broad basis of the day's pricing "bracket" which can quite adequately be done before the members meet each other across the Room. There is a body of opinion in favour of a pre-market kerb session in the Room. Whilst this would increase the facility for open bidding and offering, it would arguably also militate against the equally necessary matching-up of mutually complementary orders which can now be done between members and clients from the members' own offices.

Having completed this particular process as far as he is able, and having booked whatever back-pricing orders his clients may wish to place, each Ring member is in a position to know what he must now do in the market in order to maintain his book as he wants it. The pre-market makes it the easier for him to do just this, and to come to the Room by noon each day with a far more concise and calculated programme before him than would otherwise have been possible. This in its turn makes the final distillation process in the Ring itself the more precise, and the less disparate in terms of possibly wide differences between shades of opinion as to the day's price bracket.

Apart, therefore, from affording an opportunity for fabricators to book their permitted proportion of physical deliveries on the previous day's settlement price, the pre-market serves to match complementary orders and to bring into focus prevailing market sentiment. There will always be a sufficiently large turnover in orders expressly given for execution in the Ring for the official session to stand as the final arbiter of prices for the day. Meanwhile, the pre-market has served a useful preparatory function.

Trading in the Ring.

To the uninitiated, the Ring towards the close of an active session must seem to possess most of the attributes of Bedlam. There is no shape, no formality observable nor any apparent Master of Ceremonies. No auctioneer nor any sign of the Call Chairman who presides over trading on the soft commodity markets. The impression is one of an easy informality contrasting strangely on occasions with real tension. All this is because the Ring is self-governing: there are those in authority, and there is in fact a definite and scrupulously observed protocol. But each is embodied in the Ring itself and, therefore, neither is immediately apparent to a stranger.

During the quarter of an hour or so before 12 noon, members with their clerks and assistants drift into the market in twos and threes, pass the time of day with each other and proceed to establish contact with their own offices from their telephone booths around the Room. Comments are made on the state of the pre-market, on any other factor which is news and will or might affect the tenor of trading in the Ring that morning. As with any other gathering of professionals who know and respect each other as such, there is too a sub-current of badinage and witticisms on subjects not detectably connected with trading in non-ferrous metals. During this time, others also come into the Room and take up their stance in their habitual places. Not directly concerned with trading in the Ring, each has nevertheless his own reason and authorisation for being present. Their numbers might include principals and other executives of Ring and non-Ring companies, frequently accompanied by guests or clients whom they have signed-in (the Room is not open to the public at large), as well as a favoured few from outside such as overseas visitors or journalists: and representatives from Reuters, too.

Meanwhile the LME staff have checked that the calendars placed on two sides of the Room correctly show the day's date, as well as the three and the seven months dates. They have turned on the electronic timing device for the bell which regulates the five minute Rings, and by now one of them is standing unobtrusively by the rostrum ready to switch on the illumination of the symbols representing the five metals – placed high on the walls over the ubiquitous clocks.

The notice boards come in for a measure of scrutiny – new members elected or proposed for election, new brands of metal for registration, latest prices and warehouse stock returns: not to mention other announcements more connected with the very lively personal side of LME affairs. In short, all the small news, and the large, of a close and compact community.

At 12 noon precisely the bell rings and the symbol for copper lights up. The first official Ring of the day has started.

The subscribers and authorised clerks who are to deal in the Ring have taken their seats in the circle of somewhat venerable benches retained from the Exchange of 1881 and still contributing to the ineffable atmosphere of the LME. The seats are allocated to members by the Committee on their election to Ring dealership, and are thence-forth always occupied by the representative of that particular member company. The clerks stand behind with notebooks at the ready, for recording all deals done by their principal in the Ring. (Time was – and not so very long ago – when these clerks made a record of all trades in each Ring, but the increasing intensity of dealings, and distractions by way of telephone messages being relayed, have combined to make this task very difficult save to a few.)

Despite the hours of preparation in the pre-market as to approxi-mately (by LME standards of accuracy) where prices will emerge, the first Ring is invariably a fairly tentative encounter. A bid will be made – "I'll give two, three months" – and a counter offer "I'll sell at a half" – other voices begin to take up the threnody and for a moment there will be a flurry of vocal activity. Then, more than likely, an almost embarrassed silence during which a cough may raise a laugh or a cry of "How much?"

As though by collective telepathy, the closing seconds before the bell bring forth a mini-crescendo of calls (and by this time there will be carries offered) before the bell rings, the red symbol for copper gives way to the green for silver and dealings start all over again in another metal. A general movement as some of the dealers leave their seats, talk for brief moments before settling down again if they "have something to do in silver", and the clerks commence their rounds: checking trades just done in the copper Ring.

And so each of the five metals is traded for five minutes: silver being taken out of sequence during the first Ring in order that the first LME silver dealings may be done before the "fix" on the bullion market. The second silver Ring is taken after the day's fix is known. Each metal follows the same common pattern as to procedure, and after zinc the Room clears whilst each in his individual way savours or works through the 10 minute interval, before the second Ring commences.

Before looking at, and listening to, these very important second Rings, let us clarify something of the actual rationale of trading in the Ring of the LME. Before such dealings could be made possible at all, the contracts had to be standardised to the point where a straight bid or offer could be accepted or bargained with absolutely no room for uncertainty as to quantity or quality: the latter within the limits of the known registered brands. Place of delivery, should the buyer or his client wish to take up the metal, is in one of the number of known and approved delivery points: choice of location resting with

107

the seller. In the same way as these details were so clarified as to need no enunciation in the Ring, so had the price bid or offered, and the date of maturity of the contract (the prompt date) to be reduced to what amounts by now to an extremely precise oral shorthand.

"*I'll give Oh.*"

Only the last figure, or fraction, is called and all present are presumed to be sufficiently *au fait* with market conditions as to know already what is the "big figure". Thus, an offer of zinc at £365 50p would sound "I'll sell at a half", and a counter-bid of £365 25p "I'll give a quarter". A round figure of, say, £360 would be bid as "I'll give Oh". It is of course necessary to keep in mind not only the big figure (not always easy in moving markets, or in the tin Ring, where the last figure of a four-digit price may not on its own be very enlightening), but also the minimum fluctuations allowed. It is permitted for prices to move by not less than "quarters" (25p) per tonne in lead and zinc, "halves" (50p) in copper and pounds sterling in tin. Silver, dealt in tenths of a penny per troy ounce, is perhaps the most confusing of all the metals for the stranger to follow by ear: there being a further seven months price which is also quoted in the silver Ring.

The warehouse warrant is the standard unit of trading: 25 tonnes for copper, lead and zinc, and five tonnes for tin. Silver is traded in lots of 10,000 troy ounces. Thus for example in the lead Ring "I'll sell two warrants at six three months" after a pre-market sellers price of £214 would indicate an offer of 50 tonnes at £216. This could in turn evoke a laconic "I'll give three quarters" – £215 75p.

"*How much?*"

But there are occasions where a seller does not specify the amount he has to offer. Obviously, if he has a large tonnage to sell, to announce this and so reveal his hand could well make buyers chary and depress bid prices against him. What do do? An order to sell say 2000 tonnes "at the close" may in many circumstances be far from easy to fulfil, should the market be unresponsive. Equally, the order to dispose of the 2000 tonnes "at best" may tempt a seller to hold his order until it is too late to move it in one package in one Ring. Faced with a large selling order therefore, the dealer may simply call an offer and await developments. A cry of "How much?" from a bidder compels that bidder to take up to – but no more than – 20 warrants (500 tonnes of copper, lead or zinc) at the offered price. Should the seller not have that much to dispose of, then the bidder must be ready to take the balance up to the full 20 warrants (the "unfilled balance") from whoever immediately offers it at the price. Of course, the converse applies when a seller calls "how much?" in response to a bid.

A call of "Yes!", *tout court*, in response to an unquantified bid or offer obliges the caller to take or sell up to 20 lots from or to the other party. However, here he does not have to sell or take any unfilled balance if the 20 lots are not completed. He deals, in short, only with the one other trader and need not be at the disposal of others as well.

The LME has its conventions here too, and they are universally observed. In the case outlined above, and faced with a bid of "how much?" the offeror must not sell, say, only two warrants at the price (having in so doing satisfied himself that the demand is there) and then offer again at a higher price. Were he to do this, he would in effect be holding the rest of the Ring to ransom. Of course, if seller "A" offers and sells, and is followed by seller "B" offering (and selling) at a higher price, then seller "A" is free to offer whatever else he has now to dispose of at the newly established going price.

To make assurance double sure in such cases, both buyers and sellers are encouraged by the authorities to call firmly "I withdraw". This has the effect of converting a seller or buyer over (that is, one who still has something to do) into an uncommitted dealer still waiting for the right price at which to make his own offer or bid. It thus frees the Ring for further calling, at above or below the price at which the withdrawal was made.

Dealers in the Ring act as both buyers and sellers, and it is quite in order (and quite logical) to appear as both in one and the same call. A trader who calls "I'll give three and sell at five" is taken as meaning nothing more nor less than that – he will trade either way at the price he has named for either way. He must not therefore claim that his offer (at five) cancelled his bid by virtue of having been made later. Should he wish to withdraw either offer or bid he must clearly do so, or be prepared to deal in accordance with either.

First come, first served.
In a situation such as has been described above, there is a measure of protection for seller "A". The Rules of the LME do in fact expressly state that no other seller may offer at a higher price (nor buyer bid a lower) than that at which there is at the time another bidder or offeror. Seller "B" should therefore be certain that "A" has completed his own sale before himself coming in to offer at a higher price.

The principle of first come, first served is scrupulously observed, and an unsatisfied seller over at £250 has legitimate cause for grievance if another offers at £252 the while. This is of particular importance when the official prices are being assessed in the second Ring of official trading, and where it may well be of great importance to a seller (say) to be able to confirm that the official sellers' price was indeed that at which – on the bell – he was a seller over. He must not be put in baulk by another offeror calling a higher price whilst he still has metal to sell at the figure at which he has already offered.

Buyers too have their own measure of protection. Whilst the call "I'll take yours" by a bidder to an offeror is officially frowned upon, it does indicate readiness to buy in quantity if the metal is on offer. An offeror ought therefore not to stop – as we have seen – at say four warrants only sold to one bidder, and then after a discreet pause recommence offering at a higher price. The bidder ought to have his chance to buy what is on offer up to his own limit (provided such a tonnage is available) at the offer price originally called. If the bidder requires more, then naturally he will be ready to bid again to another seller.

Where an offer is made, and there are several bidders who by various cries of "Yes!" or "How much?" (accompanied in a busy Ring by expressive gestures indicating a strong willingness to buy) the offeror should either sell to whoever clearly was the first to bid, or parcel out the tonnage fairly amongst all. Hence, "Two for you, two for you and one for you" after an offer of five warrants has been accepted by three simultaneous bidders.

No trading limits.
Minimum price fluctuations have been mentioned. It is therefore important to make it plain that whilst these minima are adhered to, there is no equivalent maximum fluctuation. Most other markets have, and enforce, trading limits to the extent that once the price has moved up or down "the limit" then trading is actually stopped for a period. The length of such a cessation varies from market to market, and in some cases may even extend to closing the market altogether for the rest of the day.

Arguments are put forward both in favour of and in opposition to such restrictions. The LME is from time to time accused of permitting excessive daily fluctuations, and yet to impose an arbitrary limit can have the effect of locking buyers or sellers into the market – unable to purchase, or to sell – until such time as trading recommences. With the comparatively large figures involved in LME trading, and in a period of high interest rates, such enforced inactivity could well be embarrassingly expensive. Add to this the likelihood, in such circumstances, of the market reopening only to be closed once more on a further run to the limit, and it can be appreciated that what may be intended as a protection in actual fact can only exacerbate the difficulty of the situation. (The nearest approach within recent memory to any sort of trading limits being imposed on the LME was in December 1973 when an *ad hoc* decision was taken to request Ring members not to open new bought positions in zinc, either on their own or their clients' behalf. This was something of a crisis measure, taken at a time when acute physical shortage of zinc of a particular quality had brought about a sharp diminution in LME stocks and corresponding rise in the price of cash zinc on the market, with a large backwardation. In the event, the restriction was very short-lived, and trading as such hardly affected.)

If prices are tumbling, and stop-loss orders adding to the general bearishness it is surely preferable to be able to sell today – even at a loss – than to be locked-in overnight with no certainty of being able to sell on the morrow. The problem of accurate hedging against physical commitments too would be made the more difficult were a position to prove impossible to close out simply because, the market having gone up or down the limit, trading had in fact ceased for a day. Large market differences from time to time due to large price movements over the period of the currency of such a position on the market are surely by far the lesser evil.

Executions.
The facility under a principal's contract for balancing buyers with sellers outside the Ring altogether has already been noted. A further measure of the flexibility afforded by this form of contract is the discretion a Ring member may exercise in the actual execution of a contract with a client. As a simple example, the client may be a fabricator who needs copper cathodes for use in his works. He may wish to place a buying order in the Ring for a tonnage of cathodes on a future date, in order perhaps to close a hedge. Now the cathode market is not always as active as that in wirebars, and it is perfectly possible that the Ring member receiving the buying order may find himself unable to attract a seller of the date in question. In such a case he may buy the nearest available date, execute his client's order on the date required by that client, and himself cover the unavoidable

few days' discrepancy. Alternatively, since on the LME the members themselves may (and do quite properly) run positions on the market, the Ring member in this example might prefer to sell to his client warrants from his own "box", and cover in for himself at a suitable time.

These permitted – and essential – exercises of initiative by Ring members in the execution of their clients' instructions are yet another means of ensuring a completely continuous market: in which it is never necessary to plead any sort of *force majeure* as a bar to the finalisation of a deal or the meeting of a commitment. It can always be done.

The second Ring.

When dealers reassemble after the interval for the second Ring in each metal (with silver here being taken last of all), the atmosphere is noticeably different. On the last bid and offer called in each of these Rings will depend the official LME prices which will then stand as world prices for the ensuing 24 hours. Small wonder then, that a measure of tension can be felt, or that the closing seconds of each Ring are marked by an increase both in the volume and the tempo of the calling.

After the bell has sounded, one of the LME staff visits each of the three members of the Quotations Committee at his place in the Ring in order to obtain his opinion as to the final bid and offer made as the bell started ringing. After the close of silver the three "quoters" foregather in a corner of the Room for a final check amongst themselves, and to agree that in every case last bids and offers were indeed representative of the tone of prices in each Ring: not being pitched too high or too low in relation to the overall trend. This done, the Secretary or his assistant mounts the rostrum, the bell rings for silence, and the day's prices are ritually read aloud: cash and three months buyers and sellers for each metal, as well as an additional seven months price for silver.

Should there be a protest (and they are neither infrequent nor frowned on) the dealer making it stands and voices his objection: "Gentlemen, I would like to protest the three months buyers price for lead. I was bidding three right up to the bell" – or whatever his objection may be. A brief conference by the Quotations Committee follows, possibly accompanied by a groundswell of "Quite right!" from those seated around the Ring, and the decision is made there and then. Either the price is altered in deference to the

112

protest or confirmed by a polite but firm "No change, Gentlemen".

The tone for dealings, and prices, in the second Ring has been set in the course of pre-market and first Ring dealings: with the occasional exception here of silver, where the bullion brokers' fix is known after the first, but as a rule before the second Ring on the LME. After the interval therefore, it is likely that more precision (smaller brackets between buyers and sellers) will be combined with a higher degree of intensity. This applies in particular to business done on behalf of those clients, and they are the majority, who are directly concerned with the trade and to whom a shift in the LME price over the next 24 hours is a matter of great consequence. Pricing an intake or closing a hedge, when several hundreds of tons may be involved, can often be a pretty critical matter. It is here in the second Ring that individual techniques amongst the dealers, or techniques adapted to suit conditions, are observable to the experienced eye. Some may choose to contain themselves until they feel the moment critique has arrived, and then make their bid or offer; others (or the same man with a different set of conditions to deal with) may to some extent make a market by moving in and out frequently during the five minutes. All naturally seek to avoid disclosing any more of their hand than may be absolutely inescapable.

Each dealer's "card" which he carries with him into the Ring shows his positions long or short for dates where such positions exist, and it is his responsibility to make the necessary moves in order to maintain or to balance those positions at the most advantageous prices possible. Frequently an instruction conveyed in the course of a Ring may entail alteration of a planned approach: calling for extremely rapid reassessment if time (and money) are not to be lost before the adaptation is put into effect. Five minutes can be a very short time indeed, but its very brevity compels decision. In this way there is probably more intense and furious concentration devoted to the bids and offers which lead to the day's prices on the LME than applies in any other pricing forum.

The kerb market commences as soon as the prices for the day have been read. No bell, nor coloured lights now, the the market proceeds informally with trading at one and the same time in all the metals. The purposes of the kerb market are several. As has already been seen, it affords a very welcome and necessary continuation of trading for the dealer with many commitments, or many tons, to dispose of on the one date. More than this, though, the kerb offers a valuable and efficacious alternative to inter-office trading in respect of all the

113

general tidying-up of positions, of market "books", which must in the nature of things have been left unfinished on the arbitrary sounding of the bell after official trading.

To await tomorrow's official trading is to waste time and in all likelihood to miss opportunities; and the same could largely be said for a general retreat into members' own offices and a reversion to telephone trading, after the rapport which Ring dealings have only just whipped up. Additionally, as soon as the day's official prices are known then a whole spectrum of dealings – dependent on those very prices – now begins to press for attention.

As to techniques in the Ring itself, there is little outward difference from that which has gone before: save that several five-minute Rings are now extended into some half-hour of dealings, and all metals now need to be taken into account. For the individual dealer himself, it now becomes even more a matter of keeping himself abreast of minute-by-minute developments. For this reason, a call to the telephone, or however brief an interruption in order to compare notes or opinions with a fellow dealer must always be followed on his return to his seat by a query as to the latest price position overall. The Rule as to bidding higher or offering lower than others may at present may be doing is no more effective nor more important than now, in the kerb. Every dealer must now know what is being bid and offered in all metals and he must still scrupulously abide by the protocol of the market in this important respect. The sequence of offer and bid and counter-offer and bid continues with the added complication of there now being all the contracts to consider instead of only one or two. "What's three months zinc?" becomes a question which, if not asked and answered could bring the zinc market into chaos. As it is, and with such updating queries usually answered by a competent clerk, what may seem chaotic to strange ears is but a continuation of what has gone before.

In short: a continuous market demands that prices be declared once each day, to stand for that day as far as physical and direct dealings are concerned. It requires also that the dealings upon which those prices have been based should have been conducted in such a way and within such a limited period of time as to leave no ground for mistake as to their exact significance. But in the essence, and arguably the most important requirement of all, those dealings must continue throughout the intervening 24 hours with maximum contact member-to-member and minimum interruption. The place in this sequence of events taken by the kerb, as well as by the formal but still "unofficial" afternoon Rings and later still by the afternoon kerb is that of the recitative in an opera. It contributes nothing directly to the musical content of the whole, and yet without it both libretto and score would lack meaning.

Afternoon trading is in a great many respects very much akin to kerb dealings. True, the formality of dealing in separate Rings for the metals is resumed, but the atmosphere and the manner in which trading is conducted is more redolent of the informal atmosphere of the kerb than of the official dealings which preceded it. To a great extent afternoon dealings are therefore but a continuation of the morning's kerb, but there is a difference. By the time the LME has commenced its afternoon session, the Commodity Exchange (Comex) in New York is also in session. There is a considerable volume of business done in copper and silver by way of arbitrage between the two markets, and on occasions when Comex has taken a particularly definite line this can have an appreciable influence on the later LME dealings. In fact, anything so important as the closing of Comex on a limit movement up or down can have repercussions lasting beyond that day's afternoon market on the LME. Although by LME standards the amount of physical delivery business done on the New York market is very small, the amount of investment business and arbitrage with London is considerable. It follows therefore that any major movement or change in the day's trading pattern coming from that quarter will have its own reflection in LME dealings, possibly into the following day.

If afternoon trading on the LME tends to merge into the later kerb without appreciable change in tempo or atmosphere it is because the whole is effectively more of a kerb than a formalised market. Where both afternoon Ring trading and kerb come into their own is precisely when a development on the other side of the world has upset the pattern of the day's trading. Then they can act as a most necessary relief valve for the easing of any pressures generated, and in so doing provide a smoother start for the next day's official dealings.

It is as a prelude for the morrow rather than as any sort of coda to the actual day's trading, that these sessions ought to be regarded.

In sum . . .
A subject as important, at the same time as all-embracing and yet as scientifically precise as Ring dealings on the LME could – and very probably should – form the theme of an entire work of reference in itself. Unfortunately, such a work would perforce have continually

to be in course of revision. The identity of the Market as a living and developing organism is never more dramatically shown than by the constantly changing face of the Ring.

In earlier times – and yet within living memory – the dealers in the Ring were for the most part the principals in the companies represented there; in earlier, yet still recorded times those companies traded in the main, if not exclusively, on their own account as merchants. Today, the structure of businesses has altered in line with the tendency to agglomerate more responsibilities and more diverse interests within single identifiable groupings. As merchants developed into "brokers" (the word in the LME vocabulary has not quite the generally accepted meaning) and these latter into producer- or consumer-agents, so too did the producing and fabricating elements themselves start to play a direct part in trading on the LME. It could almost be said that the wheel has – or is about to have – turned full circle therefore. The difference now however, is that miners, refiners and fabricators tend to have direct representation in the Ring: whereas the erstwhile pattern was that of merchants trading as buyers and sellers on their own account. In short, the contact is once more becoming a direct one between both ends of the spectrum of demand and supply, and the number of brokers acting in that capacity is becoming less.

This puts a greater onus on the LME as a body to ensure the continuance of a viable and representative market. It also puts an onus on those who trade in the Ring today and who are by definition directly responsible for a far heavier volume of worldwide business than were their predecessors.

This tendency is not one to be viewed with unqualified delight. A leavening of independent merchants and of "old fashioned" brokers (pure middlemen) is desirable if any drift towards excessive polarisation is to be avoided. Too much influence by too few, and too easily identifiable mutually opposite forces might inhibit the very necessary flexibility of the Exchange in the completion of its work during those brief five minutes.

PART FOUR

9

Hedging on the LME

Hedging may aptly be described as a matter of holding up a mirror to physical trading. In precisely the way in which an ordinary optical mirror reverses the positions of left and right, so does a "classic" hedge reverse the positions of bought and sold. The word "classic" is emphasised because, whilst the transposition of images in an optical mirror is instant, the equivalent in a hedge on the LME is gradual, and may take any time up to the prescribed forward dealing period. There always exists the means of so adjusting the mirror as to keep the image constant – or as nearly constant as makes no matter – during this time.

In essence, a purchase of physical material for pricing on a given date in the future may be matched by a hedging sale of a like amount prompt the same date, and vice versa. Because of certain technical vagaries such as changes in the going rate of backwardation or contango, there exists both time and scope for a hedge to be modified from what may have been "classical" at the time of its opening to what may by now have become more appropriate as conditions develop during its currency. (It is really rather unfair, in this context, to separate simple buying and selling forward from the complementary technique of lending and borrowing: but for clarity's sake they will here be treated separately.)

Some of the more basic ways in which hedging – forward selling or buying – may be used in order to minimise potential loss will be the subject of this chapter. Meanwhile, certain basic principles:

1. It is not necessary to limit hedging operations to cover the actual

119

brands being bought or sold. As long as the producer prices on the LME, or his prices are so worked out as to move in line with the LME, then his brands are capable of being hedged on the market, even though they may not actually be delivered there. In the same way, any premium which may be commanded by a given brand in the physical market need not affect hedging, since it can be taken into account separately as are other incidental costs.

2. Because of the LME's facility for trading in days rather than in delivery months only, it is possible to open or close a hedge on any market day within the permitted forward trading period.

3. The fact that the great majority of producer to consumer contracts are of longer duration than the standard LME three months contract need not be an inhibiting factor. By borrowing or lending, an LME transaction may be prolonged in time in order to match producer contracts.

4. In the event of a brand registered on the LME being hedged, a possible alternative to closing the hedge by a sale or purchase on the market would be taking up or delivering the actual warrants.

5. In a thin market such as exists from time to time in certain of the metals or grades, the fact that a buyer or a seller for the precise date at the precise price may not be forthcoming is no bar. The flexibility of the LME principal's contract enables the Ring member carrying out the transaction to exercise a measure of discretion in his execution of it.

Given these essentials, some examples of how various hedging transactions are actually carried out on the LME may now be considered. In these examples, simplicity has been the main aim: in order to demonstrate how they may be done. Actual details as to other extraneous costs and cash flow are omitted: these being by no means common to all.

Selling or "short" hedge.

A merchant buys 100 tonnes of pig lead at a price based on the current LME settlement price, for shipment and eventual sale to a customer who will buy it – also at a price based on the LME settlement price – on delivery at his works. The merchant knows what he has paid his own supplier for the lead, and knows, or can with reasonable accuracy predict, his costs of freight and insurance in transit. What neither party can know at this juncture is what will be the price of lead when it is due for delivery and pricing at the customer's works?

To cover himself, the merchant will sell 100 tonnes forward (short) on the LME, prompt the date on which the physical material is due for delivery and pricing. This forward sale will be made at the price obtaining on the LME for that date.

On delivery of the metal to his customer, the merchant will buy in on the LME in order to close out his position. This he will do at the LME cash price on the day: which will also be the price upon which his sale of physical to his customer will be based. Depending on the movement in the lead price between the dates of opening and closing out the hedge, he will either receive or have to pay a market difference on the LME side of the deal. This difference will be the reverse of whatever difference there is between his original purchase price for the physical lead, and the price he receives from his customer. The two will balance (give or take whatever contango or backwardation there may have been at the time) and the merchant is covered against any adverse movement in the price of lead between inception and completion of the deal with his customer, and thus need not try to take this movement into account when arriving at his own costs and margin of profit on the deal.

Physical	*LME*
Buys 100 tonnes lead at price based on LME settlement price on date of purchase (£250) for delivery on a date within coming three months.	Sells 100 tonnes prompt on date of delivery of physical, at LME price for that date (£255.)
On date of delivery to customer's works, sells to him at the day's LME settlement price (£265.)	Buys in on the Market at same price (£265), to close out his forward sale.
Extra profit of £15 per tonne.	Market loss of £10 per tonne.

In this example, a £5 contango was assumed, and this operated in the merchant's favour as he was able to make his forward sale at a higher price than his purchase price on the Market. Selling forward into a backwardation has the opposite effect.

Had lead prices declined by £15 per tonne, the effect would have been that the merchant would have lost this amount on sale to the customer of the physical. He would, however, have recovered £20 on the LME side of the deal. Once again, the contango would have worked in his favour.

(There is a limit to the extent of a contango, but a backwardation is both without limit and very unpredictable as to its extent. For this reason, hedging into a back is treated here separately.)

The physical and the LME sides of the hedging example above are quite separate, and as the lead sold and subsequently repurchased on the LME was not intended for actual delivery to the customer, its brand and the location of the warehouse are alike immaterial.

Buying or "long" hedge.

A maker of brass rod for use in engineering is asked to quote for an order involving a tonnage of copper and zinc (the main constituents of brass). Date of delivery of the completed order is to be agreed on his customer's acceptance of his quotation. The price of the metal is the largest element in the calculation which the rod maker must now do in order to arrive at a price to quote to his customer, and in his quotation he must cover himself for whatever he must pay his own supplier for that metal. This purchase will be on a date in the future, and at prices which will be based on the as yet unknown LME settlement prices for copper and zinc ruling at that date.

The rod maker will buy copper and zinc forward on the LME (up to the amounts needed to replenish his own stock) at the current LME price for the date on which the replacement material will be required. The prices to which he has now committed himself on the LME on these forward purchases will be used in his quotation as the cost to him of the actual metal to be used in meeting his customer's needs. To these he will add his other calculated costs and his margin.

On the day he is to receive and price his replacement material he will sell against his forward purchases on the LME and close out his position there. If copper and zinc prices have risen, he will have in his favour a market difference which will offset the higher prices he must now pay to his supplier. Should prices have fallen, he will have forgone the benefit of such a fall – since the Market difference will be against him. However, in either case he will have been able to cost the whole operation from the outset without anxiety as to physical prices in the future, and to have made a firm quote to his own customer.

Had the prices of copper and zinc moved in different directions, the "swings and roundabouts" effect of hedging would still have helped the rod maker cover himself in this way.

Physical	*LME*
Copper Allows £625 per tonne as price of copper content, in preparing his quotation.	Buys 75 tonnes prompt three months hence at three months price of £625 per tonne.

Three months later, buys 75 tonnes from supplier at settlement price £585.	Sells at settlement price (£585) to close out his bought position.
Extra profit of £40 per tonne.	Market loss of £40 per tonne.
Zinc Allows £315 per tonne as price of zinc content, in preparing his quotation.	Buys 25 tonnes prompt three months hence at three months price of £351 per tonne.
Three months later, buys 25 tonnes at settlement price from supplier (£350)	Sells at settlement price (£350) to close out his bought position.
Loss of £35 per tonne.	Market profit of £35 per tonne.

The full three months period need not of course be used: if it had suited the rod maker to have used an intermediate date and price (or different ones for each metal) he could have done so. The essence is to use whatever forward price is applicable as the basic price in arriving at his quotation.

Selling hedge by a producer.

A producer may sell three months forward on the LME to hedge his own sales of physical to his customers, regardless of whether these are effected on the LME or, more probably, direct. On the prompt date he buys in to close his hedge and, if prices have fallen, his LME profit will counterbalance reduced revenue from sales of physical. If prices should have risen then the reverse occurs, but the producer has been able to cover himself against the possibility of a fall. (If he produces a brand registered on the LME he may deliver physical on to the Market rather than buy in, to close his hedge.)

On a falling market, it is reasonable to assume that there will be a contango, and this is an added incentive to forward selling on the market by a producer. Thus, assuming a 10% per annum contango:

Today cash is £600 and three months £615 (2.5% of £600). Three months hence, cash is say £560 and three months now £574.

Producer selling on basis of LME settlement price then receives £560 only for physical, but makes £55 on closing his hedge @ £615 per tonne.

Unhedged, he would have seen the cash price decline by £40 and been powerless to cover himself against this decline.

It is necessary that the producer time the closing of his hedge to correspond with pricing of his physical sale, and the problem of monthly average prices may arise in this connexion. Most producers' sales contracts if based on the LME use as their basis the average LME cash price over the month in which delivery is made. (Back-pricing is left out of account here, but covered in the chapter on pricing.)

If he has enough to sell, the producer may spread his forward hedging sales so as to include an equal proportion of the monthly total on each market day of the month: and then buy in on the corresponding days of the month in which his physical delivery is to be priced. This would presuppose a monthly tonnage of at least one warrant, 25 tonnes, per market day. In general practice however, both the forward sales and repurchases are made in one or a few tranches over the month.

Selling forward thus is attractive on a falling market and with a contango ruling. It is to a large extent unnecessary in a market where prices are rising strongly, and it becomes unprofitable when a back-wardation emerges. The producer, or his LME broker, needs there-fore to watch for signals that might forecast an upward turn in prices (*i.e.* a contraction in LME stocks) or a significant diminution of the contango. He will then have to decide whether such signs indicate a possibly lasting trend, or are symptoms only of a temporary spasm of bullishness.

Conversely, in a market which has been rising and where the pro-ducer has been content to profit by sales based on an increasing monthly average, a watchful eye should be kept on any signs that this situation is likely to change and prices to commence a downward trend. If he reads these signs aright, the producer should institute a programme of forward hedging sales at the higher levels now obtaining, in order to cushion himself against the possibility of falling revenue from sales in the months to come of physical. It may well be in his interest here to sell even into a backwardation, if that is seen to be in process of diminishing.

In view of the fact that the majority of producer contracts are for periods in excess of the three months LME contract, the need arises for hedging positions to be on correspondingly longer terms. They can be rolled forward by means of borrowing against a hedge sale and lending against a hedge purchase.

Hedging by an importer or fabricator.

Importers rarely buy physical on the LME, because under the system of sellers' options as to deliveries there can be no guarantee that they will receive the brands they require, either for their own use as fabricators or for onward sale to their customers. Indeed, some of these brands may not even be registered on the LME. Just the same, the importer who is in all probability buying his physical from producers on long term contract providing a steady rate of deliveries and pricings, wishes to keep his own purchase and sales ledgers as nearly in balance as possible for cash-flow reasons. They are not automatically self-balancing one with the other: his customers will almost certainly not themselves be buying and pricing as regularly as he is, and when possible they will opt to price at a time when the market is low, or moving in their favour.

When the importer's bought position exceeds his sold position by an appreciable margin, he may bring it into balance by selling the surplus forward on the LME. When sales have exceeded purchases, or when these forward contracts become prompt, he will repurchase them and close his position. (Note that he does not as a rule intend to deliver on the LME against these forward sales.) In the event that some or all of the forward sales are prompt whilst the importer is still long (overbought) he may roll them forward on the Exchange by borrowing: *i.e.* buying them in, and reselling them further forward.

So far, so good; and if there is a contango then the premium receivable on the forward sales will go all or a large part of the way towards covering finance and storage costs of any surplus physical he is holding in stock. (As copper is traded on the LME in warrants of 25 tonnes each, and as pricing is usually on the average LME price over the month of delivery, complete back-to-back precision is not feasible; however, an importer with a large enough throughput will tend to average-out over a period.)

Faced with the need to buy on the LME in order to match sales made outside, and in a contango, the importer would close out first the nearer dates on his outstanding LME forward sales in order to pay the least possible contango on the purchases, as well as to keep his options open as to the remoter dates against which a closing out purchase might be made at an advantageous price on a fall in market values.

Once again, the emergence of a backwardation throws these calculations out of gear. The importer or fabricator is faced with the purely subjective decision as to whether there is likely to be a fall in the price of his physical purchases which would make what now amounts to paying a penalty on his forward sales (into the backwardation) worth the paying? An extreme backwardation rarely endures for very long, since its existence at all is a symptom of a short-

125

age of nearby physical. This would either be remedied at source (settlement of a strike, resuming operations at a mine which has suffered some setback) or the shortage could well compel the supplier himself to cut back on deliveries. Unfortunately though, resumption of supplies and disappearance of the backwardation invariably bring in their wake a sharp fall in prices: "the bigger the back, the greater the fall" is a Market truism.

Should there be signs of the likelihood of an approaching backwardation – a decline in LME stocks is a reliable omen – the importer or fabricator would be advised to commence a programme of closing his forward sales in order to avoid, or minimise the need to pay the back should he close out too late.

Summing up.
The main purpose of hedging is to negate or at least minimise losses on purchases and sales of physical metal. Any extra profit which may be forthcoming ought to be regarded as a bonus – a lollipop – and not sought after as a profit in its own right. In essence, the profit or loss arising on a hedging transaction may be summarised as being the difference between cash and forward on the LME when the hedge is first set up. (Excepting here the circumstances outlined in example 2 where cash did not figure in the calculation.)

For a selling hedge, the profit or loss will be: forward price minus cash price times tonnage dealt. For a buying hedge it will be cash price minus forward times tonnage. A contango assists a selling hedge therefore and a backwardation a buying one.

Once opened, the hedge need not be slavishly kept open until the original prompt date. Advantage may be taken, and frequently is done so by the more sophisticated users of the Market, of momentary changes in prices in order to effect a partial closure: followed more often than not by reinstatement under more favourable conditions. The most important factor governing the option to do this would in all probability be a change in the relationship of cash to forward (changing contango or backwardation), rather than a change in prices overall. Taking advantage of such a change in the pattern would involve the use of carries (lending or borrowing on the Market), and will be studied in more detail in the next chapter.

10

Carries on the LME

Carries (which are comparable to "straddles" on the soft commodities markets) are put into effect by borrowing or lending. As their names suggest, these terms denote respectively buying cash or nearby and reselling forward, and the converse. In each case, both sides of the carry are done with the same counterparty, and the prices for both are agreed at the outset.

Carries may conveniently be separated into three categories, each of which is motivated for different reasons. They are: to prolong the life of a market position by rolling it forward, as a financial operation in its own right, and to square one's book in order for example to minimise interest costs on a temporarily long position. The first of these categories has been touched upon in the chapter on hedging, and it remains here only to consider certain matters of detail, which can affect the financial if not the actual tonnage content of carries.

Rates for carries.
For cash, and for each subsequent market day up to three months – and to seven months for silver – two prices are or may be quoted: buyers' and sellers'. ("May be" because it is not always certain that there would have been both bids and offers for every intervening market day. Where a price is required for a date, however, a Ring member will invariably oblige by offering to trade the date in question on the basis of buyers' and sellers' prices arrived at by extrapolation from those actually quoted for the nearest available dates.) There will always be a spread between buyers' and sellers' prices. The

smallest will be equal to the minimum step in prices quoted in the Ring, namely £1 for tin, 50p for copper, 25p for lead and zinc and 0.10p for silver. There re no maxima to spreads between buyers' and sellers' prices, and it often happens that under certain market conditions they can be quite wide: say in a comparatively inactive market, or one tending at the time to be predominantly bullish or bearish.

In negotiating a carry, each party (be he borrower or lender) must first find a counterpart who is willing to trade for the dates required, and who will make a suitable price for doing so. It is here that "Lenders Rates" and "Borrowers Rates" come into play. Taking the following prices as an example:

Cash Buyers £675	Three Months Buyers £690
Cash Sellers £677	Three Months Sellers £692

– a borrower would seek to buy at the lowest and sell at the highest; and if he were offering in the Ring he would endeavour to borrow from cash to three months at £17. In a contango, it is the lender who pays the contango and therefore in the same circumstances he would offer to lend from cash to three months at £13.

With a wide spread between buyers and sellers, and a small contango or backwardation ruling at the time, it could be that the difference between lenders and borrowers rates may be such as to extinguish altogether any purely financial advantage in a carry.

The "half and half" carry.
The spread between lenders and borrowers rates has given rise to the use of half and half carries as a convenience by Ring members. Here, the difference may be split and each party to the transaction bears, or profits by, one half of that difference. Such a carry can only be done when there is an even number of warrants in the transaction: since one rate will apply to one half and the other rate to the second half of the total tonnage carried. In this way, one or more warrants will be traded at the borrower's rate and the same number at the lender's. A half and half carry is the only instance in Ring dealing where the minimum step in prices may be disregarded and a step of half that amount bid or offered. For purposes of accounting, one half of the tonnage will be invoiced at one rate and the balance at the other so that effectively each has paid one half at the full rate.

When lending or borrowing in order to prolong the duration of a position on the Market it should be borne in mind that a change in the rate of the contango or backwardation will affect the costings of the second "leg" of the carry. This is a different situation from that obtaining in pricing further ahead than three months, and should be allowed for when hedging against such a long term pricing arrangement. It is not in fact possible to prolong a "classic" hedge beyond the forward trading limit, except possibly in a continuing contango situation.

It has already been noted, but bears repetition, that a contango being almost entirely comprised of money costs can be projected forward in time beyond three months with passable accuracy. Assuming constant interest rates, it can be taken to widen as an arithmetical progression as it lengthens in time, and changes in rates can be taken into account should they occur. On the other hand, a backwardation is almost impossible to project with any degree of confidence; though as a generalisation it can be said that the back will tend to narrow towards really distant dates. It is also likely that even within the space of three months a back will be far from uniform: often deepening sharply over certain key dates which may be critical from the physical supply and demand standpoint.

Carries as an exercise in their own right.
There could be said to be three main motives for carrying for purely financial reasons, of which the second and third are also related to the financial aspect of hedging. They are:

    1. Purely to take advantage of short term opportunities.

    2. To minimise the adverse effects of, or maximise any potential bonus arising from any change in contango or backwardation.

    3. To transfer profits or losses from one accounting or fiscal period to another. (This is a highly specialised matter in which taxation looms as important if not more so than LME dealing. As such it is outside the scope of this study, and merely mentioned in passing.)

Granted that there are usually a sufficient number who wish to lend or borrow – especially over short periods for booksquaring purposes and the like – there is rarely any difficulty in finding the other side to such an operation on the LME.

The first category above covers contango financing by banks, which has already been noted in an earlier chapter. The second might be done either as a variation of a straightforward financing transaction, or as a fairly mild form of speculation. Having borrowed into a

129

THE LONDON METAL EXCHANGE

contango and established bought price for cash, for which the warrants are now held, and price due to be received on the future sale, the borrower might decide that prices had changed sufficiently for it to be opportune to sell his bought position for cash, take his profit (and probably save himself further interest on finance), and buy forward prompt the same date as he is due to deliver against his original borrow. If he is then buying into a reduced contango (and for less than the full three months) or even with a backwardation to assist him, this step too could show a marginal profit.

Variations on the theme are legion, and carries can be a fruitful source of profit with a reasonably limited risk: provided the operations are conducted astutely. They do, however, demand constant vigilance and attention to market movements: notably to changes in the relationship of cash to forward prices. Another factor to be taken into account is that of costs. Commissions on the LME are small, but a busy book in carries presupposes a large number of transactions. The incidence of even a small element of commission will therefore be heavier than it would in larger dealings with less jobbing in and out.

A well-orientated member/client duo can, however, conduct an extremely profitable business in carries when markets are moving at all briskly.

Finally, some attention has to be given to borrowing and lending purely or mainly for the purpose of keeping a market book as nearly square as possible. This is of particular importance in times of rapidly moving prices and of course when interest rates are high. At such times, it can be expensive to be long of metal unnecessarily, and the cost of finance is appreciable even over an ordinary week-end if there is any significant tonnage being held. For this and for other reasons, a large proportion of a Ring member's daily activity is devoted to lending and borrowing across the Ring. Overnight carries are as a rule done "level": no rate will be charged and the operation regarded purely as a convenience. In other short term carries too, the price at which the metal was borrowed and lent need not actually change hands – the carrying rate only being transferred between the parties.

A further variation, and one very often done in the Ring as between members is to "borrow and lend-on" or vice versa. A member may offer, say, to borrow four warrants for 10 days from 3 March and lend-on. This means that he finds himself short on the 3rd, long on the 13th and short again on the 23rd. The transactions would look like this:

130

1. Member A buys four warrants from member B, prompt 3 March.
2. Member A delivers eight warrants to Member B on 13 March.
3. Member A buys back four warrants from member B on 23 March.

In each case, the number of warrants transferred in transaction (2) is double that in Nos. (1) and (3), and all are carried out between the same two members.

The facility for trading in named dates makes such operations feasible, and in themselves they contribute very usefully to the extreme flexibility of LME dealings.

11

Options

Trading in options is a form of speculation in price movements with a limited risk. With an anticipated rise in say the price of copper, a speculator might go long – buy forward on the assumption that when he is due to deliver against his forward purchase, the price will have so increased as to enable him to sell the position at a profit. Should he have divined wrongly, he stands to lose the difference between a high price paid for his forward purchase and a lower one realised on selling against it. This difference either way is never easily predictable at the time of the opening purchase. In order to limit his risk therefore, the speculator might decide to purchase a call option. Here, he would pay a premium to the grantor of the option and on the prompt day he may either take it up (if prices have risen sufficiently) and sell against it, or abandon the option having lost only the amount of the premium which was fixed and paid at the outset.

Risk on a short sale in anticipation of falling prices can be limited in a similar way by the purchase of a put option enabling the purchaser to sell to the grantor on prompt date at the basis price or striking price – which, like the amount of the premium, was established at the commencement.

An "each way" position can be taken with the purchase of a double option (put or call) usually at about double the premium. As the premiums required for put and call will not necessarily be the same (the amount of risk to the grantor in either case will of course differ according to conditions, as well as his own assessment of the risk of a movement unfavourable to him) so will the overall premium on a double option reflect this difference.

In circumstances where the premium on a double option is less than twice that on "call" or "put" – due to the one meriting at the time a higher premium than the other – it could be advantageous for the taker to purchase half the number of double options. One half of the double options may then be converted into calls or puts – depending on the market – and the whole "bundle" thus operate in the same direction. *For example:*

Copper calls are available at £25 per tonne premium, but doubles at £45 per tonne only (not £50). Rather than buy say 100 tonnes of calls at £2500 total premium, the taker could buy 50 tonnes of doubles at £2250 total premium. He would then buy 50 tonnes forward in the market prompt the same date and at as near to the basis price as possible.

If prices rise, then the 50 tonnes of puts (the unprofitable side in this case) are covered by the 50 tonnes bought in the market. Should prices fall, then the 50 tonnes of puts will be used in order to close this bought position.

In this way, 50 tonnes of doubles have been converted into 100 tonnes of puts or calls – depending on price movements – at a saving of £250 in total premium.

As a rule, buying options will only be a fruitful exercise in its own right if prices are moving widely; the premium paid is irrecoverable, and therefore the price on the declaration day (when notice of the intention to exercise the option must be given) must have moved up or down by an amount larger than the premium plus commission and any interest incurred for an overall profit to be shown on the deal.

LME options are traded in the same contract lots, and for periods up to the same maximum forward dealing periods as are ordinary purchases and sales of warrants on the market. (Individual arrangements as to longer periods may be made if the market justifies this, although they are always in months rather than in dates.)

In outline, the procedure is for the purchaser ("taker") and the grantor of the option to fix the basis price at which the warrants will eventually change hands if the option is exercised. The premium is agreed and as a rule paid over to the grantor at the commencement. The amount of the premium in relation to the basis price will vary according to backwardation or contango rates ruling at the time, and the grantor's own assessment of likely market movements during the currency of the option. The grantor has to minimise the financial risk to himself, without the contrary risk of pricing himself out of the market.

133

The purchaser of the option must make his declaration (that he intends to take it up) in writing to the grantor before noon on the declaration day. This date will be set out in the contract, and as a general rule on the LME it will fall on the same number of market days before prompt date as there are months in the total period of the option. Failure to make a formal (affirmitive) declaration is taken automatically as abandonment of the option and consequent forfeiture of the premium.

At its simplest therefore, purchase of a call option confers the right to buy (call for) the warrants on the prompt date at the basis price. If prices have risen over and above the cost of the premium plus incidentals then a profit for the purchaser ("taker") ensues. If prices fall, or do not advance far enough, his only loss is the premium and these incidentals. The converse applies to a put option, which confers the right to sell to the grantor at the basis price.

Trading against options.

To buy an option and then await results may often be frustrating, as prices see-saw, or obstinately remain within too limited a bracket. It usually pays therefore, to trade against options already bought.

Taking a call as an example, having bought one or more call options prompt three months (and it rarely repays the effort to trade only in singletons rather than multiples), the purchaser now has a position against which he can sell up to the same number of warrants without actually being caught short. He has bought the right to call for delivery of the warrants on the prompt date and so is in a position to sell or if the market is volatile to job, in a like number of warrants.

This facility is of importance not only in producing a further marginal element of profit – effectively recouping some if not all of the premiums paid – but as a means of limiting potential loss of a more serious nature by actually converting a call into a put, or vice versa. The taker of a call may very soon see that he has in fact bought his option at too high a price in the light of a downward trend now developing on the market, and that he is now therefore on what appears to be an automatic loser – unless there be a lucky reversal of the trend. He may take advantage of this movement though, by selling short on the market against his options. Had the trend been in his favour at first, and then fallen away, and had he been astute enough to note this in time and make his short sale at or above the basis price of the options then he would for practical purposes have converted a call into a put, and on a falling market.

Such active market dealing against established options can greatly increase their effectiveness: especially when prices are moving and there are appreciable short term differences in contango or back-wardation rates. It is very necessary to ensure that at no time does the number of warrants traded against options exceed the number of the options themselves, lest an uncovered position arise.

As in any other form of forward dealing on the LME, a contango will militate in favour of a put – or sale on a future date – when it is likely that a purchase for cash or nearby against this sale can be made at an advantageous price. The converse in principle would apply to a backwardation, when the forward purchase (the call option) could in due course be liquidated by a sale for cash at a premium. However, a back usually infers unstable prices and may even presage a sharp fall ("The bigger the back, the bigger the fall"), and by the prompt date the market might have declined sufficiently for the cash sale not to be profitable. Great vigilance, in whatever market operation is in train, is always essential when there is a backwardation ruling.

Granting options.

This is a very specialised operation, and the grantor must at all times see himself covered: both as to taking or making delivery should the option be exercised, and as to his resulting position if it be aban-doned. He needs therefore to ensure considerable room for ma-noeuvre against either contingency. As a rule, options will be exercised only if the price has moved in the taker's favour, and the grantor must therefore be covered against having to deliver or take up warrants in a market not necessarily favouring such a course. Against a call, he should already be long at the right price, or against a put have a taker for the warrants which he will himself acquire should the purchaser (taker) of the option see fit to exercise it.

A holder of physical stocks (importer or fabricator) may well be in a position to grant options via a Ring member. He may either deliver from his own inventory or take into inventory as the case may be, and either way he will hedge his own position as a holder of stocks on the market by one of the hedging methods already out-lined. Granting options, more than any other method or technique of trading on the LME is essentially a matter of judgement: here, not only of prices and trends, but of exposure. As such, the exercise should be treated with a proper respect.

12

Pricing

There are two major sides to the pricing of metal on the LME: use of the official settlement price as the basis for purchases under a contract from a producer, and use of the market for the purpose of establishing, or protecting, a price for future deliveries or sales by dealing forward.

Contracts for physical material between producer and fabricator or importer.
Unless there is a set producer price in operation, the vast majority of contracts for deliveries over a period are priced on the basis of the average LME settlement price during the month of shipment of each batch of material. Over the years however, the tradition has emerged of producers allowing their larger customers – or those taking a fairly regular tonnage over each contract year – to price an agreed proportion of their intake against the LME settlement price announced the day previous to that on which a shipment is due for pricing on the terms of the contract. This facility is known as "pricing terms" or "back-pricing", and it is important in that it affords to the importer an opportunity to make a hedging profit as an offset against an adverse trend in the average prices, as well as to quote a firm price for a given day to any of his own customers. Under typical pricing terms an importer could secure to himself the option to price up to, say, 25% of his monthly intake on any one day: at the previous day's LME settlement price. There would additionally be a limit placed on the frequency of his exercising this option within each month: say

not more than 50% of a month's total in any one week. (Under these particular terms, an importer could in fact price his whole month's intake "on the known" by pricing in two tranches in two successive weeks.)

In order to price thus, it is necessary that the instruction to do so is given before the commencement of official trading – 12 noon – on the day of pricing. Once official trading has started the previous day's settlement price has no further significance in this regard, and the importer must now wait until today's prices are announced, if he still wishes to price on the known.

Pricing terms are much valued by importers and fabricators: not least because they are thus themselves given a marked amount of latitude as to the actual sums they will pay over each month. They are also put in the position of being able to confer a similar privilege to certain of their own customers, and because of the way in which they facilitate hedging, the granting of such terms is an undoubted sales aid.

In a case where an importer has back-priced say 250 tonnes of his producer intake to yesterday's settlement price, and then seen today's price come out at £10 per tonne higher, he has automatically won himself a bonus of £10 per tonne on a resale at today's price. To cover himself against a possible fall, however, it would be prudent for him to sell a like tonnage forward on the LME at the moment he books the 250 tonnes for his own intake. Thus:

10 June   Settlement Price £650   Three Months £630.

11 June at 11.00 a.m. importer advised that market appears to be rising, so books 250 tonnes at £650 (yesterday's settlement price) and sells 250 tonnes prompt three months on LME – now trading (11 June) at £635.

12 June settlement price announced is £665 and three months is £635. Importer sells to customer at £665 (today's price) and buys in three months sale at £635.

Profit on physical is £15 per tonne, and zero on hedge.

If the market had turned after the back-pricing and hedge sale on the eleventh, and settlement price come out at £640, with three months at £625, then the importer would lose £10 per tonne on his physical sale through having misread the market, but would recoup £10 per tonne on his hedge: thus safeguarding his overall position.

The whole system of back-pricing may appear to be one of the illogicalities in an otherwise mathematically logical marketing process. It was introduced at a time when the major primary producers were keen to tie their customers up to contracts extending over a period – usually one year at a time – and when prices were such that some sort of sales aid was manifestly desirable in order to achieve this. After taking advantage of back-pricing terms, the larger importers were not slow in passing on a part of this advantage to their own customers; it would now be hard to see the system readily abandoned after having become to some extent hallowed by tradition.

Other aspects of using the LME as a medium for establishing a price have been touched on in the chapter on hedging, but there remain some further examples which are worth a little attention.

If frequently happens that material must not only be ordered but also priced some time before delivery. (This is different from pricing on an unknown settlement price on date of delivery, which has already been noted.) Terms for pricing in advance of delivery vary from case to case, but two that are fairly typical would be the option to price on the known settlement price at date of placing order, or to price on an as yet unknown settlement price at an agreed date between placing the order and delivery of the material.

In the first instance, the purchaser would book for delivery say three months hence at the known LME settlement price of the day previous: thus establishing a firm price for the material from the outset. He may, however, be selling his own product based on LME prices current at the time of such sale. He must therefore cover himself against a possible fall in prices between now and date of delivery of physical to him, and pricing the material to be contained in his own product. This he would do by selling a like tonnage on the LME prompt the date of delivery of the physical. A fall in market values will enable the purchaser to recover the difference when he closes this short hedge, and costs his own sales on the basis of the later LME prices ruling at time of these sales. On a rising market, he would lose on the hedge but recover on sale to his own customers, based on the ensuing higher price.

Conversely, should the purchaser price on an unknown LME settlement price midway (say) between order and delivery, yet be required to give a firm price as of now for his own future sale, he would execute a buying or long hedge. Here, he would price his own sales on whatever figure he was able to buy forward at in the market: prompt the date agreed for pricing the physical delivery to him.

By using the LME thus, the purchaser has been able in the first instance to cover himself against risks on pricing his intake now, and pricing his products in the future. In the second instance he has established a firm price for the finished product now, despite uncertainty as to the eventual cost to him of the metal to be incorporated in it.

Variations on the theme are legion, but the basic principle of covering on the market remains valid. Further complications are introduced when there are options to price on either cash or forward prices: here contango and backwardation must be allowed for, and the principle observed that buying forward into a back, and selling into a contango are the more profitable options.

Example.
Pricing on unknown six weeks forward for delivery three months forward, and making firm quote to own customer *now* on a sale due three months forward.

Result.

Date	LME Official Prices	Operations with Supplier	Operations on LME	Operations with Customer
15 March	Cash – £680	Orders metal for delivery on 16 June – to be priced on LME cash quote on 30 April.	Buys forward, prompt 30 April at £665.	Quotes him a firm price of £665 for delivery 16 June.
	3 months £650			
30 April	Cash – £720	Prices intake at £720	Sells cash at £720 – Closing his forward bought position (at £665).	—
16 June	Prices are are now immaterial.	Intake delivered, and paid for at £720.	—	Sells to his customer at £665

(*a*) Bought metal from supplier at £720 – a notional loss of £40 per tonne between LME cash price on day of *ordering* (15 March) and day of *pricing* (30 April).

(*b*) Made profit (real) of £55 per tonne on his LME operation. Thus his actual net cost was £665, being the £720 paid to his supplier *minus* the £55 profit on the LME hedge.

He may now calculate his own costs and margin on the operation, having safeguarded himself from any uncertainty as to price of the material.

13

Settlement Price

As the settlement price forms the basis for all transactions carried out on the LME, as well as for pricing a very high proportion of direct producer to consumer trade, some words of explanation and enalrgement are called for. In so far as direct dealings are concerned, a producer in one country who sells ores or metal to a consumer in another must have some point of reference upon which a mutually acceptable price can be established. The daily LME settlement price forms such a datum; each party to a direct over-the-frontier deal may base his own calculations on this known (and published) factor.

The LME prices are announced after the close of official trading on every market day; and this announcement includes the settlement price, which in point of fact is the same as the cash sellers' price on the day. It has a double significance. Outside the LME, settlement price is taken as the reference for contracts based on LME quotations and now due for pricing. It is also taken as that day's component in any arrangements for pricing on the average of LME quotations over a prearranged period of time. Thus, the settlement price is very widely accepted as the base price for sales of physical metal which are not actually done on the Market at all.

Deals which have been done on LME contracts, and which are now prompt, are all concluded at settlement price. Differences either way between this figure and the individual contract prices – perhaps negotiated as long as three months beforehand – are then calculated and shown separately in the account.

A typical LME Ring member's account to a client might look as follows:

Brand	Pieces	Weight	Rent		
XYZ	220	25,034	24/9/75	1 week	
XYZ	221	24,999	24/9/75	1 week	
		50,033		2 weeks	

At £428 per tonne in warehouse London.	£21,414.12
Less Rent at 12p per tonne per week.	6.00
	£21,408.12

Contract Price £431 per tonne	
Settlement Price £428 per tonne	
Difference £ 3 per tonne	150.00
	£21,558.12

Although this method appears unnecessarily complicated at first sight, it is logical in that the difference between present prices and original contract prices is at once apparent. Anyone having taken the step of buying or selling forward will have an interest in this difference (hedging, profit-taking, etc.). It also makes far easier the handling of contracts between Ring members which have been cancelled-out as to actual delivery by execution of counter-contracts for identical tonnages and prompt date.

If these contracts were entered into at different times in the three month period before the prompt date (and in all probability with different counterparties as well) it follows that they will have been made at differing prices. If member A had bought 100 tonnes for 20 June from member B on 21 April and then sold 100 tonnes for 20 June to member C on 15 May, there would be little point in his collecting the warrants from B and paying him for them, and straightaway handing them on to C and collecting from him.

The LME "clearing" here comes into play as a method of dealing each day with deliveries between Ring members in respect of all contracts now prompt. The notion of the clearing originated as long ago as 1890, and the form in use up to the present was the brainchild of the ingenious Mr. Neems (a Committee member) in 1909. It is perhaps best described by way of example, showing how the movement both of large sums of money and of valuable warehouse warrants may be reduced to a minimum. The saving in time, cost and the risk of misplacement of documents of title is obvious.

Before 6 p.m. on each market day every Ring member must provide the LME Office with a clearing form in respect of each metal: showing tonnages to be delivered to, or taken up from, each other Ring member with whom he has contracts prompt the day following. At the foot of the forms he indicates the overall total he is due to take up or deliver. Note that no mention of prices is made on these forms. The staff in the office collate the returns early the following morning and direct members due overall to deliver to make their deliveries to those due overall to receive. In this way it is possible – indeed almost certain – that a Ring member will transfer warrants to or from another with whom in fact he had not done any business for that particular prompt. It has simply happened that the one is due overall to deliver and the other to receive: their own original counterparties having in the interim closed out their positions by buying or selling for that date.

All transfers of warrants under directions of the clearing are effected at the previous day's settlement price. Differences between this and individual contract prices are then dealt with separately, and directly between the parties concerned without intervention by the clearing. The effect of this procedure is for the first seller in any chain of deals to deliver warrants to the last buyer at the settlement price, whilst all in the chain settle between themselves as to any difference between this amount and their own contracted prices.

The essential distinction between this "clearing" and a full Clearing House is that at no time is anyone's contractual obligation shifted on to anyone else. Individual contracts stand as such for the various prompt dates – there is no provision for early "washing-out" – and differences between settlement price and contract prices remain the responsibility of the members concerned as and when they arise.

Example.

In one three month period:

A sold to B 100 tons @ 600 per ton = £60,000
B sold to C 50 tons @ 620 per ton = £31,000
B sold to D 50 tons @ 650 per ton = £32,500
D sold to A 50 tons @ 660 per ton = £33,000

Therefore on prompt date

A is a net seller of 50 tons
B is square as to tonnage bought and sold
C is a net buyer of 50 tons
D is square as to tonnage bought and sold

On prompt date, the settlement price (SP) is £700 per ton.

A delivers 50 tons to C and receives £35,000 = 50 × £700 SP
  receives difference from D of   2000 = between contract price £660 and SP
                                           £700 × 50 tons.

                                   ————
                                   37,000
He pays difference to B of   10,000 = between contract price £600 and SP
                                           £700 × 100 tons.

                                   ————
He gets net   £27,000 = proceeds of 100 tons sold @ £600,
                                   ————   less cost of 50 bought @ £660.

B No delivery or take-up of warrants
  He receives difference from A of £10,000 = *see above*
  He pays difference to C of   4000 = between contract price £620 and SP
                                             £700 × 50 tons.
  He pays difference to D of   2500 = between contract price £650 and SP
                                   ————   £700 × 50 tons.

He gets net   £ 3500 = proceeds of 50 tons sold @ £620 and
                                   ————   50 at £650 less cost of 100 bought
                                             at £600.

C No delivery of warrants, but takes up 50 tons from A
  He receives difference from B of   4000 = *see above*
  He pays A   35,000 = 50 tons at £700 SP

                                   ————
He pays out net   £31,000 = cost of 50 tons at £620.
                                   ————

D No delivery or take up of warrants
  He receives difference from B of £ 2500 = *see above*
  He pays difference to A of   2000 = *see above*

                                   ————
He gets net   £   500 = after purchase at £32,500 and sale
                                   ————   at £33,000

The procedure as a rule works well enough, and undoubtedly saves time and expense. However, difficulties can occur should, for example, a member take up warrants via the clearing where there may be a defect as to title, or as to quality or quantity of metal covered by those warrants. In such a case, he may have taken them (on instructions from the clearing) from another member with whom he was not in a contractual situation and therefore to whom he has no recourse should there be any such defect. The rarity of such *contretemps* does not entirely outweigh the disadvantages of the system in this respect, and there is a strong school of thought that warrants ought to be delivered to and collected from a central "pool" with its own insurance arrangements.

14

Value Added Tax, Exchange Control and Other Outside Influences

The prospect of value added tax being introduced in the United Kingdom in 1973 was viewed by all the London commodity markets with some justifiable apprehension. With the facilities offered by the markets for buying and selling for future delivery and with the more or less complete unpredictability of the prices at which forward contracts would be settled, the problems appeared to be insoluble. From the practical standpoint too the sheer weight of numbers of transactions (many involving the same parcel of merchandise as it was traded on the market prior to a future delivery) would bring in its train an intolerable accounting burden. Furthermore, anomalies would inevitably arise if tax were to be accounted for at the same rate and at the same time on a market transaction – closing a hedge for example – and on the physical side of the hedge: which could have been contracted at a quite different price.

The problem was basically to ensure that both physical and market sides of hedging and comparable transactions were taxed on the same footing, whilst at the same time ensuring freedom from tax accounting for all the myriad market deals. As shown in the example, the exemption from VAT of any transaction or class of person, far from solving this problem, simply makes it the more fractious.

VAT is in essence a turnover tax with provision for deducting sums already paid to suppliers in the course of business ("inputs") from tax now due to be remitted to the authorities from payments of VAT received from customers in response to one's own invoices ("outputs"). Each registered trader collects tax from his purchasers, deducts whatever he may himself have paid to his own suppliers, and accounts for the difference with the authorities.

The ultimate purchaser for consumption (retail) not being registered pays VAT and may not reclaim this. Thus, as an easy mnemonic:
"Your inputs are your outgoings, your outputs are your income, if
you are registered for VAT you do not pay it (you pass it on) and if
you are unregistered you do pay it."

The scheme ultimately adopted for the commodity markets by
agreement with HM Customs and Excise – the authority in the UK
responsible for VAT – was made possible by the recognition in
Britain of VAT at "zero rate". This is absolutely logical, and simply
means that tax is chargeable, but at 0%. Under such a category, it is
possible for a trader to reclaim or set off any VAT paid by him as
inputs in his own settlements of his own suppliers' invoices, yet at the
same time not to invoice his own customers for VAT – save at 0%.
If he has a net credit balance of inputs over outputs at the end of
each accounting period (usually three months), he may reclaim direct
from the authorities.

Having agreed the principle on which any such scheme might rest
(and granted zero rating to make it possible at all), it remained only
to delineate the actual limits of the concept of each market – within
which it would be permissible to trade all contracts at zero VAT. Note
from the example, how essential is the distinction between "zero
VAT" and "no VAT at all" – the interposition of a VAT-exempt
stage in a series of transactions has the effect of causing the transaction immediately preceding it to be taxed twice over. Here, the
representatives of the markets and of HM Customs maintained long
and detailed discussions, and in the event a remarkably simple basic
pattern was arrived at.

Material being brought into a market must be so brought with
VAT accounted for. Material being sold out of the market must
similarly be sold with VAT accounted for at the price at which that
sale is made. Material being bought and sold within the market may
be traded at zero rate VAT. Thus, there is no accounting problem in
dealing with VAT on very numerous purely market deals (carries
etc.), whilst at the same time inputs (costs) may be allowed for VAT
in market hedging deals in just the same way as are allowed on their
physical counterparts.

Before reviewing how this procedure actually works on the LME –
and unfortunately, a measure of understanding of it is now pretty
essential – the following example with VAT conveniently fixed at
10% will show how the basics work out.

Example 1.

Stage 1.	A sells to B	@ £500	VAT (Output)	£50	*less* A's Input	£ –	*equals*	Net VAT to Customs £50
Stage 2.	B sells to C	@ £550	VAT (Output)	£55	*less* B's Input	£50	*equals*	Net VAT to Customs £ 5
Stage 3.	C sells to D	@ £600	VAT (Output)	£60	*less* C's Input	£55	*equals*	Net VAT to Customs £ 5

Total Outputs £165   *less* Inputs £105   *equals* Net VAT to Customs *£60 on £600*

Example 2. (B is exempt).

Stage 1.	A sells to B	@ £500	VAT (Output)	£50	*less* A's Input	£–	*equals*	Net VAT to Customs £50
Stage 2.	B sells to C	@ £550	sale exempt	£ –	no Input allowed to B			No VAT on this stage
Stage 3.	C sells to D	@ £600	VAT (Output)	£60	no Input claimed by C		*equals*	Net VAT to Customs £60

Total Outputs £110   No Inputs claimable   *equals* Net VAT to Customs *£110 on £600*

Note: Because B (exempt) could not claim input on VAT he paid to A, this sum was not deductible from total VAT – effect is as though first sale were taxed twice.

Example 3. (B is zero rated).

Stage 1.	A sells to B	@ £500	VAT (Output)	£50	*less* A's Input	£ –	*equals*	Net VAT to Customs £50
Stage 2.	B sells to C	@ £550	sale zero rated	£ –	*less* B's Input	£50	*equals*	Net VAT to Customs *minus* £50 (B's Input)
Stage 3.	C sells to D	@ £600	VAT (Output)	£60	*less* C's Input	£ –	*equals*	Net VAT to Customs £60

Total Outputs £110   *less* Inputs £50   *equals* Net VAT to Customs *£60 on £600*

Note: Balance restored at final stage, since B (zero rated) was able to claim input on VAT he paid to A.

This is how the VAT procedure works on the LME:

1. *Getting metal into the Market* – whence all deals involving it will be zero rated until the metal is taken out of warehouse for consumption.

(*a*) Member imports the metal and puts it on warrant in an un-bonded warehouse in the UK. He is due to pay import VAT on the metal: this is at the same rate as domestic VAT, though it is payable on the total price after any Import Duty has been added. Being registered for VAT, the member may claim in his VAT return for any import VAT paid, as an allowable "input". The two entries in his return, import VAT payable and input allowable, counterbalance each other and no money need actually be paid by him to the authorities.

(*b*) Member purchases metal already on warrant, but from a seller outside the LME. This could either be UK production bought from the producer, or material already imported and now bought from the importer. In each case, VAT or import VAT will already have been paid, and the LME member will receive a VAT invoice from his supplier. The member has to pay this VAT to the vendor since the latter must account for it in his own return. In this case, by arrangement with the authorities, the LME member may claim the amount he has paid direct from them as an input.

(*c*) Member purchases metal on warrant in a warehouse outside the United Kingdom. There is no VAT problem here, as the material at this stage is outside the scope of VAT in the UK.

The metal is now inside the market, and for as long as it remains thus, it is zero rated for VAT in all subsequent market dealings. It will not again be subject to the tax until it is sold out of the market, when the VAT will be based on that final selling price.

Since warehouse rents in the UK are themselves subject to VAT, it is necessary for metal already on warrant to be bought into the market with rent paid up to date, and VAT on the rent accounted for.

2. *Dealings inside the Market.*

(*a*) All sales between members are VAT-free as regards price. Accrued warehouse rents may continue to be rolled forward and allowed for on invoices, following standard LME procedure which has already been noted, as though there were no VAT on the rent.

(*b*) A member sells to a non-member. As long as the metal remains in warehouse and is not actually taken up, this sale is zero rated.

(*c*) Similarly, a member may buy metal on warrant from a non-member at zero VAT, where the latter himself had bought it at zero VAT from a member of the LME. (Since all transactions to which one of the parties is an LME member may be zero rated, it follows that a non-member could buy from one member and resell to another within the market for VAT purposes.)

On the LME principal's contract, the zero rate provisions can be carried no further: in (b) above any subsequent sale by the non-member to another non-member automatically comes outside these provisions and VAT must be accounted for in the usual way *regardless of whether there is physical movement of the material or not.*

In dealings in silver, the market concept is taken further, to include named members of the London Silver Market and named Ring members of the LME in the one whole as far as VAT on silver transactions is concerned.

3. *Getting metal on warrant out of the Market.*
(a) Sale to a non-member of metal on warrant in a UK warehouse, and the client wishes to take up the metal for use within the UK.

(i) The member must account to the warehouse for the rent (which will have been allowed to him up to the date on which he himself acquired the warrant), as well as VAT on the rent for the whole period during which the metal has been on warrant and "in the Market". This the member will do against a tax invoice issued by the warehouse.

Thus the member will pay the rent from the date on which he got the warrant (rents prior being allowed him in the invoice he paid when he himself bought the warrant), but he will pay VAT on the rent for the whole period the metal has been on warrant. Being registered, he may claim this as an allowable input against other outputs, so there is no penalty.

The member now may sell the warrant "clean".

(ii) The member now has to account for VAT on the price. He issues a tax invoice to his purchaser, and accounts for VAT paid by his purchaser as one of his outputs.

(iii) Finally, he must affix either an LME or a London Silver Market certificate to the warrant, confirming that VAT on the price has been accounted for, and this will authorise the warehouse to release the metal.

(b) Non-member has already bought at zero VAT in the market, but he now wishes to take the metal out of warehouse for physical use within the UK.

(*i*) In unbonded warehouse, the non-member must sell to a member and immediately repurchase from him – both deals are done for convenience at the day's settlement price. His sale to the member is still inside the market and therefore zero rated for VAT. Resale to him by the member will be out of the market – at his request, as he has signified that he wishes to take up the metal – and the VAT accounting procedure outlined above will be followed. In this case, rent will be paid up to date of the non-member's sale to the member, so as to be up to date on the resale to the non-member.

(*ii*) In bonded warehouse, the only procedural difference is that VAT on the price (not on the rent) be paid direct by the non-member purchaser in the last deal to HM Customs, as from their standpoint he has just imported the material. All export sales are currently zero rated in the UK.

(*c*) Where the metal has remained the while in a continental warehouse, there are no VAT complications as to rent: the purchaser will account for VAT on the price according to the laws of his own country.

So much, in brief – very brief – for a rather large subject. It is worth bearing in mind that in matters of taxation no two cases are quite alike; and after assimilating the principles of the procedures on the LME it would still be wise to consult one's own advisers as to one's individual position, be it as a company or an individual.

European Common Market duties and tariffs.

With an appreciable domestic production of lead and zinc, the EEC seeks naturally to protect its own producers of these metals from the more adverse effects of imports at uncompetitive prices, and for this reason a tariff is imposed on all imported lead and zinc over and above a set duty-free import quota. (These quotas are based on a member-by-member formula, with an additional "community quota" for contingencies; they are to be phased out by 1978.) As a sort of counterpart to the EEC tariff, though historically older, there remains the vestige of a duty on these metals imported into Britain from other than Commonwealth countries. This is a hangover from the days of Empire Preference. This tariff also will be phased out over a similar period, though the process may be accelerated at the initiative of the UK Government. Both duties are for fixed amounts per tonne: the EEC Common External Tariff (CET) being at 13.2

Units of Account, and the UK duty at £1.476 per tonne (formerly £1.50 per long ton.) A "Unit of Account" is the purchasing power of one US dollar in the currency of the country concerned.

Neither duty is applicable for as long as the material remains in duty-free or freeport warehouse: being attached only on uplift of the metal for use within the Community, or on its being placed in an unbonded store. Paradoxically, the present situation is that all continental warehouses registered by the LME are duty-free (or "offshore" in one way or another for duty purposes), whereas the great majority of those in the United Kingdom are domestic in that duty must be paid on depositing goods there.

As they stand based on a flat rate per tonne, the duties present no problem to LME trading. For UK warehouses (duty paid) the flat sum is merely passed from hand to hand as warrants are transferred on the market, and for metal in continental warehouse a purchaser knows in advance what he must pay if he wishes to take the metal into use. However, it is the aim of the EEC Authorities eventually to put these duties (plus one now at a lower figure, for lead bullion) on to an *ad valorem* rather than per tonne basis. This could indeed cause problems in terms of LME trading and pricing. It is in a sense fortunate that to date – due to increased prices for metals – GATT consent has not yet been forthcoming for making the change.

As the nearest feasible approach to solving a basically insoluble problem (on what price would an *ad valorem* duty rest – LME settlement on date of uplift, or on date of last purchase maybe months or even years ago, or on individual contract price of that last purchase? Or on price at which metal was first placed on warrant – again probably some long time ago?) the LME contracts for lead and zinc were recently altered. The old condition that "duty if any is for buyer's account" was simply deleted along with the old list of registered warehouses for lead and zinc. The effect of this is that any question of payment of duty or of the premium that may be its equivalent in respect of EEC production be a matter between the final importer out of bonded store and the authorities. A case perhaps of ignoring a problem in the expectation that it will then go away, but it has the effect that all metals are traded on the LME on a completely ex-duty basis – as is the case with VAT. The LME price remains a completely neutral one.

Another problem arising out of the EEC system of protection is that of the quotas placed on tonnages of metal (notably lead and zinc) which may be imported from the Comecon (Eastern) Bloc countries in any one year. Here unfortunately there arise anomalies between the situation affecting different EEC warehouses themselves. In Rotterdam, for example, metal is stored in Transit Warehouse. Here it may rest free of duty or premium and at the same time free of any import or export restrictions. In other words, EEC production may be placed on warrant in Rotterdam and subsequently taken into use inside the EEC with no problem: production from outside the Community would be free of restriction provided it was within the quota when placed in warehouse. In the free port area of Hamburg on the other hand, all material lodged there being outside West German customs territory counts as though "exported"; it must therefore be subject to full import procedures if it is to be brought into Germany for use. And this includes quota restrictions. This is somewhat illogical, and in an important sense it places Hamburg and possibly Bremen at a disadvantage if only in terms of procedures to be gone through when taking up EEC production from warehouse there.

Exchange control – the Bank of England.

The reopening of the tin market on the LME in September 1949 was indirectly the cause of the initiation of the now familiar "F E Scheme". Arrangements had to be made whereunder LME members and their clients were freed from some of the more irksome restrictions in connexion with foreign exchange control, in return for their assumption of certain obligations – for the most part concerned with making a regular disclosure to the appropriate department of the Bank of England as to their own and their clients' foreign exchange position on Metal Exchange commitments.

LME members were, and continue to be admitted as members (participants) in the scheme on the recommendation of the Committee, which in its turn assumes a measure of responsibility for ensuring that the requirements of the Bank in this regard are duly met. As "The Executive", as defined in the official memorandum of the scheme, the Committee are answerable to the Bank for the proper conduct of members' affairs from the exchange control standpoint, and for the rendering by members of the monthly returns to the Bank.

Joining the scheme is effected quite simply by the member making application advising the Committee through the Executive Secretary of the names of his nominated bankers for foreign exchange purposes. This information is then passed to the exchange control department of the Bank of England, who make contact with the nominated bankers and in due course advise the Executive Secretary that formalities have been completed. Once in the scheme, every member must abide by its requirements: and of these possibly the only irksome one is rendering the monthly return – delay in which results in a sharp exchange of letters between the Bank, the Executive Secretary and the dilatory member.

Essentially, the scheme enables LME members to purchase metals in any part of the world, as well as store and tranship them. Payment is then made in sterling to an external account, or in foreign currency. Sales likewise may be made to any national and the metal in issue may be lodged in any registered LME warehouse.

There is a clause in each of the LME clients' contracts to the effect that in the event of sale to a UK resident of warrants covering metal outside the UK the purchaser will abide by the conditions of the scheme; and a simple form is provided for completion by seller and buyer in such cases. The scheme also permits the transmission of market differences; members may maintain sterling accounts in their own books in the names of their non-resident clients, and (with Bank of England consent) accounts also in foreign currencies for purposes of such dealings. The scheme covers forward purchases and sales, arbitrage with overseas markets and the nominated banks may issue, confirm or advise credits connected with dealings covered by the scheme.

Application of the scheme to silver dealings when that market was instituted in 1968 has already been noted: there is still a separate return in respect of silver, though the other metals are aggregated on one single form.

A truly international market must at all times endeavour to be neutral in all its dealings, and especially in respect of prices: which must not be affected or coloured in any way by local conditions or restrictions. Complete achievement of this aim is probably impossible but the LME has contrived to go a very long way towards it. Credit for this fortunate state of affairs must be shared between the management of the market itself and the authorities in the United Kingdom – notably the Bank of England – who consistently display an encouraging appreciation of the LME's aims, and of its value to the economy in general.

Postscript

In common with every other trade organisation the LME finds itself in a constant process of evolution. Just as it has come a very long way from the formative days in the Jerusalem Coffee House, so the Exchange continues along this sometimes devious and never very clearly signposted road. Leaving aside the almost continual changes in detail as to procedures and techniques, what forecast might be made as to major shifts in outlook, policy and business transacted?

Without a doubt, the matter of the internal security of the market and the mutual accountability of its members looms very large. Some brief mention has already been made of the likelihood of changes in procedures in order to move further in this direction: though it would at this point in time be premature to make any attempt at a precise definition of what may emerge. It is however, most unlikely that new developments along this path will alter in any significant way the essential rationale of the LME as a principals' market attuned to the needs of the trade. In brief, any alteration will be of a technical nature rather than one of principle.

As to additions to the range of metals traded on the LME it is unlikely that anything like the old pig iron market would ever be revived: though the emergence in 1975 of a free market in steel in London may point the way to a move towards closer liaison (to put it no higher) between that market and the LME. Of the other essential metals, aluminium has more than once been the subject of intense study: most recently in 1971-72. However, on each of the several occasions when a potential aluminium market has been canvassed, the project has foundered on the lack of any assurance that sufficient "chips" in the form of metal freely available for trading would be forthcoming in such a highly integrated producer-to-consumer field. Curiously, the avowed support of merchants and secondary (as opposed – almost literally – to primary) producers in Europe seems not to have persuaded the LME quite to take the plunge. The same basic problem, added to domination of the market by producing interests, was found to apply to nickel when an in-depth investigation was made in the latter part of 1970. Changing conditions in the markets, or in the economics of marketing from the primary producers' standpoint could each very quickly bring the LME searchlight once more to bear on either or both of these metals.

The "minor metals" perhaps present a more attractive potential. For many months in 1971 and 1972 the topic was under review by a Sub-Committee set up for the purpose. Lack of standardisation of grades and shapes (the latter also an obstacle in the way of an aluminium contract), as well as the very wide diversity in contract and delivery terms seemed to make a traditional LME Ring in any of the minor metals unworkable. However, there was a strong faction on the LME in favour of admitting trading in some at least of these metals – antimony, mercury, tungsten are examples – rather along the lines of the old lead and zinc dealings before these metals were traded in the official Rings. The project never proceeded very far and in due time the Minor Metals Traders' Association was established separate from the LME. It would seem now that the opportunity to introduce some of these metals to the LME via some form of secondary Ring has receded, although the way is still open.

Another recurring theme in LME thinking is the registration of delivery points for metals traded under LME contracts in locations both geographically and economically more widely spread than the present nexus in the United Kingdom and on the North Sea seaboard of the Continent. There are extremely strong trade and consumer links with the eastern seaboard of the USA as well as with Japan; and there are links too with Africa, Australia and Latin America. What is the likelihood of LME warehouses in all or at least some of these areas, to say nothing of warehouses within the European hinterland? In principle, and as leading to a wider spectrum of trading, the arguments in favour are both easily understood and hard to resist. Unfortunately, geography in terms of voyage times as well as foreign exchange problems tend to make the situation more difficult – or at least more subtle – than it might at first appear.

An easy answer – and one which might well serve for a time at least as an interim measure – might be to recognise some or all of these more dispersed areas as delivery points whose warehouse warrants were marketable at a fixed and known discount *vis-à-vis* those on locations closer to hand. The problem of course goes very much deeper than merely that of time taken in shipping to or from these areas, and until some sort of formula has been worked out which will take floating currencies into account it is hard to see how a viable trade in these warrants could be sustained. To this difficulty should be added that of providing for the comparatively free movement of metal when a very wide geographical area may be affected by political or other disruption at national or international level, rather than a narrower one bounded closely by unaffected areas themselves housing delivery points: such as is the position in Europe now as far as it affects the LME warehouses.

This said, the argument is so strong as to be virtually undeniable that one of the greatest single factors in the stabilisation of prices would be the establishment of LME warehouses in many more areas – centres of production as well as of consumption. The underpinning of surplus stocks by financing operations, and the existence reasonably near at hand of a "float" of largely independently financed stocks when demand turns upwards are alike vitally important stabilising forces. The more profuse the distribution of warehouses holding these stocks, the more will local (in world terms) imbalances of supply and demand be containable.

Unfortunately, the unfettered movement of metal is not the only criterion; there are also reasons why the provenance of that metal – or of the warrants conferring title to it – must assume an importance. In times of surplus a very high proportion of stocks of metal in warehouse is carried by interests not directly involved in the LME as a purely financial operation – contango financing – and this forms one of the main supporting buttresses under the prices when trade interest may for one reason or another be temporarily at a low ebb. Any financial institution holding LME warrants at such a time and for such a purpose must be able to rest secure in the knowledge that those warrants are freely negotiable, or interchangeable, and to dilute such a vital mixture with the addition of less attractive warrants would be a most debatable course of action. Thus, a spread of delivery points must be matched with a measure of selectivity as to the international acceptability of warrants emanating from such points from the banker's point of view.

155

And – membership? The logic behind the requirement that Ring members should only represent companies registered in Britain and with more than a set proportion of British Nationals on their boards has been under fire for some time. Already the various "head-quarters" and other fiscal arrangements between countries have made the domestic taxation argument less tenable. Meantime, EEC ties draw its members closer by degrees. The many and various inter-governmental moves in the direction of bringing the laws of contract, of arbitrations and other procedures closer into line also point towards the feasibility – sooner rather than later – of permitting international membership of what is already known and respected as a truly international market.

Appendix 1
Glossary

Arbitrage: Dealings whose profitability depends on the difference in price between one market and another, or between one currency value and another. Typical LME examples would be buying copper or silver in London on the LME and offering in New York on the New York Commodity Exchange (Comex). Dealings in silver may also be arbitraged between the LME and the bullion market.

Arbitration: All LME contracts, as well as many contracts for metals not necessarily traded on the LME, provide for any dispute arising to be settled by the appointment of two or occasionally three arbitrators. It is important to note that arbitrators act as independent umpires and *not* as advocates for one disputant or the other.

Assay: Analysis of metals submitted in order to arrive at confirmation of their purity. May be done by any of several methods (spectroscopy, etc.) and produces a list of other elements found in the sample, and their percentage of the whole.

ASTM: The American Society for Testing Materials. The official body in the USA for laying down standards as to purity as well as methods to be adopted for sampling and assaying.

Authorised clerk: Anyone admitted as such on the LME and thereby authorised to deal in the Ring on behalf of his employer. The status

157

is purely an LME one, and the individual's status in his own organisation is for this purpose irrelevant.

Back-pricing (*see also* Pricing terms): A regular customer of a smelter or refiner or other supplier may be permitted to price a proportion of his month's intake on the known LME settlement price quoted the day previous to the date of pricing the intake. The proportion to be so priced is laid down in the contract, and the consumer – if he wishes to avail himself of the facility – must place his order before commencement of official trading on the LME on the date in question.

Backwardation (often abbreviated to "Back"): Denotes the premium of cash or nearby dates over three months or remote dates. There is no limit to a backwardation.

There is a theory that when the market is in equilibrium as to supply and demand, a backwardation is a logical state of affairs: since producers selling forward in order to hedge their own anticipated supplies to the market will expect to pay a premium in order to do so. Consumer hedging will of course work in the opposite direction. None the less, it is probably true that in "ideal" conditions as to supply and demand a modest backwardation should be expected.

NB. Both Backwardation and Contango (*q.v.*) may show peaks or troughs for various dates within the forward trading period for which they are expressed. They do not necessarily progress in a straight line from cash to three months.

Bear: One who anticipates a fall in market values.

Borrowing: Buying cash or a nearby date and re-selling further forward. Both transactions are done at the same time and with the same counterparty, at prices and for dates agreed at the outset. A borrower pays a premium if he borrows into a backwardation, and receives a premium should he borrow into a contango.

BSI: The British Standards Institute. The official body in the United Kingdom for laying down standards as to purity as well as methods for sampling and assaying metals.

Brand: All metals deliverable on the LME must be of a brand registered as "good delivery" by the Committee. Brands, of which there may be many produced to different specifications and of different qualities by any given smelter or refiner, are as a rule identifiable by some distinguishing mark.

Bull: One who anticipates a rise in market values.

Buyer over: A bidder who is still unsatisfied (*i.e.* still calling his bid) at the close of a Ring. An unsatisfied buyer. If he is the last such, then his bid will be the official buyers' price for the day, in the Second Ring.

Carries: The generic term for borrowing and lending, or a combination of the two. A carry may be extended for up to two weeks beyond the three months time limit applied to buying and selling operations.

A carry is frequently used in order to roll a buying or selling trade forward in time, rather than take (or make) delivery on the original prompt date, or close-out by executing a trade in the contrary sense. It is essentially an exercise in fluidity, since changing contango or backwardation rates will apply.

Cash: A contract on the LME for settlement and for delivery (of warrants) on the day following.

Cash today: A contract between Ring members for settlement the same day. This must be done before 12.30 p.m. on the day in question.

Clearing (not to be confused with a Clearing House (*q.v.*)): The market mechanism whereby sellers overall deliver to buyers overall at the ruling settlement price. *See* Settlement Price for detailed explanation.

Clearing house: May be either an independent body, or one owned by members of the market in question. A clearing house registers all contracts done in the market, and may substitute one party for another by novation. Thus if a trader has both bought and sold the same number of lots for the same delivery month (not trading days as on the LME) he may drop out of the transaction as the clearing house matches his original counterparties with each other.

The clearing house also guarantees fulfilment of every contract registered; and as a safeguard calls for an initial deposit (fixed throughout life of contract) and further margins from those with open contracts where prices are moving against them. Favourable price movements would give rise to a return of margins, but in practice those doing a large or regular turnover tend to have a regular credit line with the clearing house for this purpose, supported by guarantees or by collateral.

Closing out: Execution of a contract for a date and tonnage which will cancel a previous obligation by matching it as to date and tonnage (though not price, where difference is treated as the profit element on the deal). On the LME it is necessary to await the prompt date before closing out, whereas with a Clearing House (*q.v.*) it may be done when the second contract is entered into.

Commission house: An institution, often of international coverage, which places orders with members of the exchanges on behalf of its own clients. Clients' individual purchase and sale orders may be aggregated, and form part of larger orders which the commission house then places in its own name. Several commission houses are non-Ring members of the LME.

Consumer (*see also* Fabricator): Any organisation taking in bar, slab or ingot as traded on the LME and converting it to other forms of finished or semi-finished products. Not to be confused with one who buys and may hold warehouse warrants but never actually takes up the metal for use.

Contango: The premium commanded by three months or remote dates over cash or nearby dates. It expresses the costs of carrying metal over the period and therefore has a definite limit; *i.e.* money costs plus warehouse rent plus insurance.

Contract price: The price agreed between the parties at which an LME contract is entered into. Margin on Prompt Date (*q.v.*) between this figure and the official Settlement Price (*q.v.*) is the market Difference (*q.v.*).

Contract weight: The LME contracts provide for delivery of set amounts (25 tonnes for copper, lead and zinc; 5 tonnes for tin; 10,000 troy ounces for silver). There is a clause in the contracts which allows up to 2% either side of the exact contract weight as good delivery.

Custom smelter: An organisation refining into bar, slab or ingot from materials (*e.g.* blister copper, scrap, concentrates, etc.) provided by others who then take back the refined shapes. The custom smelter derives his profit from the "returning charge" on these activities.

Delivery point: A location (usually a port) approved as such by the Board of the Company, on recommendation by the Committee, within which one or more registered warehouses are located. Many factors – geographical, economic, etc. – may determine the choice of a delivery point which, therefore, becomes a matter of LME policy, hence sanctioned by both Board and Committee.

Difference: Trades are done between the parties at the agreed contract price. Deliveries of warrants in respect of trades done are effected at the settlement price ruling on the prompt date of such delivery. Margin (if any) between settlement price and the original contract price is a difference and is accounted for separately.

Trades closed out before prompt date and which do not result in any transfer of warrants will as a rule result in a difference: the margin of profit to one party or the other.

Execution: Under the LME principal's contract, a Ring member may deal with a client at a price agreed between them, specified by the client or left in any of several ways to the discretion of the member. In the event that the member is not able to obtain the exact price in the Ring for the date and tonnage in question, he may none the less execute with the client at the agreed price, and bear any difference himself.

Fabricator (or sometimes "Semi-fabricator"): A Consumer (*q.v.*) who is in business to convert bar, slab, ingot or cathode, etc., into finished products or into semi-fabrications such as rod, extrusions, angle or tube.

Hedging: Covering a forward commitment in physical metal by entering into an equal and opposite commitment (in terms of tonnage and prompt date) on the market. Loss on the one will be equated by profit on the other.

Inter-office trading: Name loosely given to bids and offers between Ring members made on the telephone each day before official Ring trading commences. Whilst this period undoubtedly affords Ring members an oppportunity to "test the market" it has possibly an opposite effect in that such trading is not done in the full publicity of Ring dealings. In fairness it must be said that quite a volume of business may be done in this way, on more or less accepted prices (give or take negotiation) which would otherwise have unnecessarily cluttered official Ring dealings.

Kerb trading: Dealings in the Ring or in the Room, and therefore done in the open market, between Ring members, yet outside official or the afternoon "unofficial" but still formalised market.

Kerb dealings have significance in that they enable a Ring member perhaps to complete business either interrupted by the Bell in official trading or which might have been too large in volume for a particular official market to have contained without an effect on prices. They are also a very large part of the essential flexibility of the LME in that they provide time, opportunity and market for the multiplicity of book-squaring transactions which ought to be done before a day's business is closed.

Lending: Selling cash or a nearby date and repurchasing three months or at a remoter date. The converse of Borrowing (*q.v.*).

Lifting a leg: Closing-out one half of a back-to-back deal such as a lending or borrowing. The trader is now uncovered to the extent of the remaining (open) commitment.

Long (Going long): Buying forward on the market, and thus being "long" of metal for a given date. May be a speculative position in anticipation of rising prices when the bought position may be closed-out by selling advantageously, or may be a market position taken against a contrary physical commitment.

Options: These make it possible, on payment of a premium, to buy (call) or sell (put) on the declaration day at the basis or striking price agreed when the option was taken out, or to abandon the option on forfeit of premium only should the market not respond to the forecast of the taker of the option. In this way, potential losses on an adverse price movement may be limited to the amount of the premium.

Pre-market: Dealings between Ring members (and between Ring members and their clients) done largely by telephone before official trading commences. An important part of member to client dealings will be on account of clients exercising back-pricing facilities.

The confidentiality of such dealings may, it is argued, militate against the sort of full disclosure which would otherwise have facilitated pricing in the open (official or kerb) market.

Pricing: Using official LME price (or a formula based on the average of such prices over a period) as the basis for purchase price of physical metal.

Pricing terms: *See* Back-pricing.

Producer: May refer to a miner, *i.e.* a producer of ores or concentrates, or to a refiner of these into ingot or other merchantable form. In this latter sense also covers converters of scrap into secondary metal.

Prompt date: The date (always a working day) on which a forward LME contract becomes due for settlement.

Seller over: An offeror who is still offering at the close of a Ring. (*See* "Buyer over".)

Semi-fabricator: A producer of semis (or semi-finished products).

Semis: Metal which has been fashioned into any of a number of recognised shapes – tube, angle, etc

Settlement price: The official cash seller's price at the close of the second Ring of official trading. Is used as basis for trades in physical metal done outside the LME, as well as for internal accounting purposes on all LME trades now prompt for settlement. (In such cases, difference between settlement price on prompt date and the original contract price is separately accounted.)

Short: Sold forward. The converse of Long or Going Long (*q.v.*).

Stocks: Metal on warrant in a registered LME warehouse. LME stocks (of which the total amount is published weekly) are *not* the property of the Exchange, but of the holders of the warrants at the time.

Stop loss: A buying or selling order placed in advance, which has the effect of cancelling out a previously contracted selling or buying order (the two are indeed often placed at the same time). On the LME a stop loss must always be executed at exactly the price stipulated by the client.

Warehouse: Any location having covered storage, with adequate security provided, which has been inspected and approved by the LME for registration as an approved warehouse. Warehouses may be in several categories, *e.g. free-port* or "outside customs territory"; *bonded* or "within customs territory" yet able to hold goods on which import duty or import-VAT have not yet been levied; *transit,* which is comparable to bonded; or *inland,* where duty, etc., has been paid on goods stored.

Warrant: Document of title issued by warehouse conferring title to set parcel of goods (*see* LME warrant weights) to person named on face of the document. Warrant may at any time be endorsed to another nominee or to "bearer" – making it a readily negotiable document from the standpoint of its use as collateral for bank finance etc. Warrants are the accepted documents on the LME and as such may change hands rapidly during trading on the market – secure in the knowledge that the underlying security (the metal) lies in warehouse and available to the current holder of a warrant.

White contract: Name given to contracts between LME Ring members and clients in respect of physical metal for forward delivery – frequently over periods extending well beyond the three months life of the standard LME contracts.

Appendix 2
Ring Trading Times

A. Official
1200–1205 Copper (wirebars and cathodes)
1205–1210 Silver
1210–1215 Tin (standard and high grade)
1215–1220 Lead
1220–1225 Zinc

1235–1240 Copper wirebars
1240–1245 Copper cathodes
1245–1250 Tin (standard and high grade)
1250–1255 Lead
1255–1300 Zinc
1300–1305 Silver
Official prices for the day are quoted after the last of the above Rings.

B. Unofficial
1535–1540 Lead
1540–1545 Zinc
1545–1550 Copper (wirebars and cathodes)
1550–1555 Tin
1555–1600 Silver

1605–1610 Lead
1610–1615 Zinc
1615–1620 Copper wirebars
1620–1625 Copper cathodes
1625–1630 Tin (standard and high grade)
1630–1635 Silver

Appendix 3
LME Registered Brands

COPPER BRANDS

Official list issued by the Committee of the London Metal Exchange of the brands and descriptions deliverable in fulfilment of contracts for Copper.

Wirebars
Electrolytic copper in the form of wirebars of standard dimensions in the weight range of 90 kg to 125 kg.

Australia	Brands—ISA
Belgium	UMK
Canada	CCR—ORC
Chile	AE—ENM— ◇ CCC / MR
Congo	UMK
France	PAL
Germany (East)	MEK
Germany (West)	HK—NA—WEK
Japan	HM—Mitsubishi—OSR—SE1—SR—KRR—FNR
Peru	C de P—C P Peru
Poland	HML—HMG
Portugal	CUF
South Africa	PMC
Spain	CEM—ECSA
Sweden	Boliden Koppar
United Kingdom	E★R—RCB

USA	ALS—BER—B & M—DRW—LNS— (NEC) —
	PA—P★D—T
USSR	MI
Zambia	MCM—NCR—REC

High conductivity fire refined copper in the form of wirebars of standard dimensions in the weight range of 90 kg to 125 kg.

Germany (West)	NAFR
United Kingdom	BCR—ERM
USA	AMCO
	RHC

Cathodes

Electrolytic copper in the form of cathodes assaying not less than 99.90% of copper (*silver being counted as copper*).

Australia	ISA—Erands
Austria	Brixlegg
Belgium	ME—UMK
Bulgaria	MK
Canada	CCR—ORC
Chile	ENM
Finland	OKM
France	PAL
Germany (East)	MEK
Germany (West)	CF—HL—KER—NA—WEK
Hungary	CSMW
Italy	ATC—Rifometal—SMI
Japan	Dowa—HM—Mitsubishi—Mitsubishi 0 Mitsui—OSR—SR—Sumiko—Dowa Okayama—Tamano—FNR
Mexico	CDM
Norway	FEC
Peru	C de P ⎯⎯⎯ Peru C P Peru
Poland	HML—HMG
Portugal	CUF
South Africa	PMC
Spain	CEM—ECSA—Indumetal—RTP—SIA MYC
Sweden	Boliden Koppar
United Kingdom	Actid—ELK—Enthoven—JB Melton Cathode Copper—RCB (max size 44″ × 36″)—MKB

USA	BER—DRW—LMC—PA—RMR—T—CME— —Magma—CDS
USSR	MO
Yugoslavia	Bor
Zambia	Mufulira—NCR—REC

Fire Refined
Class A
High grade fire refined copper assaying not less than 99.88% of copper (*silver being counted as copper*) in the form of ingots or ingotbars.

★★★

Chile	MB—MR
Germany (*West*)	BKR2—NA
S. Africa	MTD
S. Rhodesia	MRSR
United Kingdom	EFF—JB—MC3—MX—PRE
USA	Q—R

Class B
Fire refined copper assaying not less than 99.70% of copper (*silver being counted as copper*) in the form of ingots or ingotbars.

Belgium	MF
Germany (*West*)	BKR1
United Kingdom	BE BS DE—E—GMU—JBBS Mersey—PRE75—Yellow Spot MXY—WBMR

TIN BRANDS

Official list issued by the Committee of the London Metal Exchange of brands of Tin deliverable in fulfilment of contracts for Standard Tin and High Grade Tin. High Grade Tin brands are deliverable against the Standard Tin contract.

Tin deliverable against the Standard Contract and the High Grade Contract shall be in ingots or slabs not less than about 12 kg nor more than about 50 kg.

Standard Tin

Australia	Pyrmont
	OT Lempriere & Co.
Congo	Geomines
Denmark	Bera Refined Tin (Lion with Ox-head)
Federation of Malaya and Singapore	OTS
Germany (*East*)	F

Germany (West)	M—Standard
	NA
	Zinnwerke Wilhelmsburg
Netherlands	Tulip
	Windmill Star
Portugal	Embel
Spain	Concha
	Mesae
	Reina Isabel B
United Kingdom	Associated Lead
	Chempur
	Cornish
	Hawthorne
	Penpoll
	River
	W H & Co. Mellanear

High Grade Tin

Australia	ATS
	ATS Low Arsenic Refined Tin
Belgium	UMHK
Brazil	Trevo
	Bera Brasil
	Best
	Cesbra
	Mamore
Federation of Malaya	ES Coy Ltd Straits Refined Tin
and Singapore	Straits Trading Company Limited
Germany (West)	M—Spezial
	Rose
	Tree
Indonesia	Banka
Netherlands	Billiton
	Windmill I
	Windmill II
	Windmill III
Nigeria	Makeri
Spain	Concha A
	Mesae 99·9
Thailand	Thaisarco
United Kingdom	Pass No. 1
	Pass USA Grade A
USA	Double Circle
	GCMC
USSR	XXX

LEAD BRANDS

Official list issued by the Committee of the London Metal Exchange of brands of Refined Pig Lead deliverable in fulfilment of contracts for Standard Lead.

Refined Pig Lead deliverable against the Standard Contract shall be in pigs weighing not more than 50 kg each.

Australia

◇ BHAS ◇ Broken Hill Australia ◇ Special ◇

BHAS Lead 99·97

◇ BHAS ◇ Broken Hill Australia ◇ BHAS ◇

Belgium
Campine ER
Hoboken Extra Raffine
MCR Made in Belgium
★★★Veille Montagne★★★
99.97%+Fabrique en Belgique 99.97%+

Bulgaria
K U₁ M
O U₁ 3

Burma
BM Refined

Canada
Tadanac

Denmark
Bera

Eire
MRL

France
Penarroya

Germany (East)
F

Germany (West)
Braubach Dopp Raff B (Deutschland)
BSB
Eschweiler Raffine
Harz W 99.97
NA (Norddeutsche Affinerie) F 99.985
NA (Norddeutsche Affinerie) E 99.99
NA (Norddeutsche Affinerie) H 99.97
Raffiniertes Harz Blei
Stolberg

Italy
AT & C
Monteponi
Pertusola

Japan
Dowa
ESS
TAK
EMK—K
EMK—T
SK
Three Diamond

Mexico	Asarco
	CMFyAM Mexico
Morocco	PZ Maroc
Netherlands	Saturnas
	Tulp
North Korea	KM
Peru	Cerro-Peru
	C de P Peru Industria Peruana
Poland	C P Peru Industria Peruana
	H2OMS
S.W. Africa	TCL
	Tsumco
Spain	Cia La Cruz-Linares-Espana
	Guindos Doble Refinado
	Penarroya Importe d'Espagne
	RCA
Sweden	Bera
	Boliden A
	Boliden B
Tunisia	Penarroya Tunisie
United Kingdom	Afco
	Associated Lead
	BLM
	BL Co
	DX
	"Emo"
	GMU
	H J Enthoven & Sons, L^{td}
	LAA
	Melton Refined Lead
	PM
	Holyrood—Thames 99·99+ —
	"HM" Lead 99197%
USSR	Ykcuk
Yugoslavia	Trepca
Zambia	Sable 99.99+
	ZBHD
USA	Bunker Hill
	Glover
	M
	Omaha and Grant
	Rainbow
	Revere
	Southern Star

ZINC BRANDS

Official list issued by the Committee of the London Metal Exchange of brands of Virgin Zinc deliverable in fulfilment of contracts for Standard Zinc.

Virgin Zinc deliverable against the Standard Contract shall be in slabs, plates or ingots weighing not more than 50 kg each.

Australia	AZ
	Derwent Prime
	BHAS PW
	BHAS 99.95+
	BHAS 99.99+
	A-Z PW
Austria	BBU 99.99
Belgium	Prayon
	Rothem
	UO Raffine
	★★★VM Fabrique en Belgique
Bulgaria	H P b
	K U₁ M
	H P b
	O U₁ 3
Canada	Hudson Bay Special High Grade Zinc
	Hudson Bay High Grade Zinc
	Hudson Bay (Prime Western) Zinc
	Tadanac (Prime Western)
Finland	Outokumpo
France	Penarroya Z6
	RCA Special
	SMMP
Germany (East)	F
Germany (West)	★★★Altenberg
	DKH
	Fah. Harz Zink 98.5
	Harz Zink 99.5
	Huettenzink Harz 99.5
	MHD
	RMZ
	SS
	Weser Extra Raff
	Wesser Zink 98.5
Italy	Elett MP
	Monteponi
Japan	M M C M S C
	‾H‾ M S C R I

	M M C	T O H O
	$\overline{M}$	
	SK	
	SK SHG	
Mexico	Rosita	
	Contimex	
	Zincamex	
	Penoles	
Netherlands	Campine	
North Korea	KM	
Norway	Norzink Elektro	
	Norzink Elektro 99.99+	
Peru	Cerro-Peru	
	C de P Industria Peruana Peru 99.99+	
	C de P Industria Peruana Peru (Prime Western)	
	CP Industria Peruana 99.99	
Poland	Polsk Raf	
	EO	
Rumania	Zn D 1	
Spain	EDZ	
United Kingdom	Avonmouth	
	Imperial Avonmouth Smelting	
	Imperial Severn Smelting	
	Imperial Swansea Vale Smelting	
	MS	
	Severn	
	Swansea Vale	
USA	Amarillo	
	Amax	
	Amco (Prime Western)	
	Amco-Blackwell	
	Bunker Hill	
	Granby D	
	Lehigh	
	Meadow Brook	
	M & H	
	PI	
	St Joe	
	Asarco Electro	
	National— $\boxed{\begin{array}{c} \text{NZ} \\ \text{ZN} \end{array}}$ —HNP—PSN	
USSR	Ykcuk	
	UB	

Yugoslavia	Celje
	Zorka
	Zletovo
Zambia	Sable 98.5+

SILVER BRANDS

Official List issued by the Committee of the London Metal Exchange of brands of Silver deliverable in fulfilment of contracts for Silver.

Silver deliverable against the Fine Silver Contract shall be in the form of bars in the weight range 450 to 1250 troy ounces.

Argentina	Stella
Australia	BHAS
	ESA
	Erands
Belgium	Société Générale Métallurgique de
	Hoboken SA
	Hoboken 999.7+
	Hoboken 999+
Bulgaria	M
Burma	Burma Mines
Canada	CCR
	ORC
	Tadanac
France	Comptoir Lyon
	MBLG
	Compagnie des Métaux Précieux
	Heraeus
Germany (East)	Mansfield
Germany (West)	Degussa
	Norddeutsche Affinerie
Italy	MP
Japan	Three Diamond
	Dowa
	NSS
	HM
Mexico	Asarco-Monterey
	Cia Minera de Penoles SA
	Cia Metalurgica Penoles SA
	Metalurgica Mexicana Penoles SA
	R del M
	SAM
Netherlands	Smelting Schones
	HDZ
Poland	ZTM

Peru	C de P
	C P Peru
South Africa	RRLd
S.W. Africa	TCL
Spain	Orispania
	Peñarroya
	Socemp
Sweden	Boliden Silver (999)
United Kingdom	BL Co
	JM
	JMC
	JMCF
	Johnson Matthey London 999
	JSCF
	JSW
	R
	SS Co
USA	Asarco-Baltimore
	Asarco-Perth Amboy
	Asarco-Selby
	AS & R Co-Baltimore
	AS & R Co-Perth Amboy
	Selby Gold & Silver Refinery, San Francisco, Cal.
	Balbach
	BER
	Bunker Hill
	DRW
	E
	ISR
	KUE
	Raritan
	Seal of the USA
	S-M
	UMS Co
	USS Co
USSR	CCCP
Yugoslavia	BOR
	Trepca

Appendix 4

Example of LME Contract

Authorised 19th February 1975

COPPER WIREBAR CONTRACT FORM

**Approved by the Board of Directors and by the
Committee of the London Metal Exchange**

Contract B

LONDON...,

M...

$\dfrac{\text{I}}{\text{We}}$ have this day $\dfrac{\text{sold to}}{\text{bought from}}$ you according, and subject to the
Rules and Regulations of the London Metal Exchange.

....

....Tons (two per cent. either more
or less and subject to Rule 3 below) of

176

COPPER–WIREBARS

Price £...per ton of 1000 kilogrammes

net $\dfrac{\text{plus}}{\text{minus}}$ .... % to us

The appropriate Import Duty (if any) ruling on the prompt date to be for Buyer's Account.

Prompt ....

    We have the right at any time on demand to require you to pay us such a sum (hereinafter referred to as a "margin") in cash and/or to deposit with us security in such other form and of such amount not exceeding the value of the contract as we in our discretion require and in order to secure the due fulfilment by you of your obligations under this contract and to the intent that the value of the margin in relation to the contract shall at all times during the currency of the contract be maintained by you we have the further right on demand and whether in one or more calls to require you to pay to us the difference between the value of the contract at the time of entering into the same and the current market value at any time thereafter as we in our discretion require. In the event of any failure by you to fulfil your obligations we have an immediate right of appropriation of any such cash and/or to sell any security to satisfy our rights as above in addition to all other rights reserved to us by this contract.

This contract is made between ourselves and yourselves as principals, we alone being liable to you for its performance. The percentage (if any) charged by us to you is to be regarded simply as part of the price and may be shared by us with agents introducing the business, whilst we reserve the right also to charge a percentage or commission to any person from or to whom we may have bought or sold to cover our liability hereunder.

In the event of your failing to meet your engagements arising out of this or any other outstanding contract or contracts between us which are subject to the Rules and Regulations of the London Metal Exchange whether by failing to provide on the due date documents to meet sales or money to take up documents (as the case may be) or otherwise howsoever or of your failing to supply or maintain such margin (if any) for which we are entitled to call and have called or in the event of your suspending payment or becoming bankrupt or committing any act of bankruptcy or (being a Company) in the event of your going into liquidation whether voluntary or otherwise, we reserve the right to close this contract and any other said outstanding contract or contracts if as and when we in our sole discretion shall so decide by selling out or buying in against you (as the case may be) and any differences arising therefrom shall be payable forthwith notwithstanding that the prompt day or other day originally stipulated for settlement may not have arrived.

Any delay in our enforcing any of our rights under this contract shall not be deemed to constitute a waiver thereof.

Members of the London Metal Exchange

SPECIAL RULES FOR COPPER WIREBARS

1. Quality. The Copper delivered under this contract must be in the form of wirebars of standard dimensions in the weight range 90 kgs to 125 kgs, and may be either:—

(a) Electrolytic Copper

or

(b) High Conductivity Fire Refined Copper

In the latter case (b) a deduction of £20 per ton shall be allowed on the invoice.

All Copper delivered must be of brands approved by and registered with the Committee, and must conform with the current appropriate standard of either the BSI or the ASTM.

2. Settlement. Contracts shall be settled on exact quantities of 25 tons at the official Settlement price quoted by the Committee operative on the prompt date, Buyer and Seller paying or receiving, as the case may be, the difference, if any, between the Settlement price and the contract price.

3. Delivery. The Copper shall be delivered on the prompt date in warehouse; either London, Birmingham, Manchester, Liverpool, Birkenhead, Hull, Newcastle-on-Tyne, Glasgow, Avonmouth, Swansea, Rotterdam, Bremen, Hamburg (free port area) or Antwerp in seller's option. In all cases the warehouse must be one approved by and registered with the Committee. Warrants tendered in fulfilment of contracts shall be invoiced at the Settlement price mentioned in Rule 2 above in parcels each of 25 tons or a multiple thereof (each 25 tons to be treated as a separate contract). Warrants shall be for 25 tons each (two per cent either more or less). Warrants issued prior to the 1st January, 1970 for long tons shall constitute good delivery provided that their weights are within a 2% tolerance of 25 long tons. Each parcel of 25 tons shall be of one brand, shape and size, and shall lie at one warehouse. Rent shall be allowed on the invoice.

4. Weights. The word "TON" wherever appearing in this contract shall be a metric tonne of 1000 kilogrammes. In the case of warrants where weights are shown in long tons conversion shall be at the rate of 1 long ton to 1016 kilogrammes. Warrants weights in all cases shall be accepted as between buyer and seller.

5. Warrants. Each Warrant must state the brand and whether electrolytic or HCFR and the wirebars comprising each parcel of 25 tons shall be of uniform weight subject to the usual tolerances, and the wirebar weight and the number of wirebars comprising each parcel must be shown on the Warrant.

6. Exchange Control Regulations. If Rotterdam, Bremen, Hamburg or Antwerp warrants are delivered to a resident of the United Kingdom not participating in the Bank of England Metals Scheme in fulfilment of this contract, the seller must issue a CM form in accordance with the procedure currently in force under the Scheme. The buyer must conform with the requirements expressed on those parts of the CM form which he receives from the Seller.

7. Disputes. Any question concerning formation and any dispute under this contract shall be notified to the Secretary of the London Metal Exchange in writing by the seller or the buyer or both of them jointly. Such question or dispute if not settled by agreement shall be referred to arbitration in accordance with the Rules and Regulations of the London Metal Exchange. The decision in writing of the Appeal Committee from the Award of the Arbitrators shall be a condition precedent to a Notice of Motion to remit or set aside the Award of the Arbitrators and the decision of the Appeal Committee or to an action being brought. The Uniform Law concerning the formation of contracts for the International Sale of Goods and the

Uniform Law regulating the International Sale of Goods shall not apply.

(In the above Rules "The Committee" means the Committee of the London Metal Exchange)

CONTRACT RULES

Rule A. Members of the London Metal Exchange, in their dealings with other Members, shall be responsible to and entitled to claim against one another, and one another only, for the fulfilment of every Contract for Metals.

Rule B. In these Rules the expression "Members of the London Metal Exchange" includes Firms and Companies who, although not themselves Subscribers to the Exchange, are represented and deal thereon by and through "Representative Subscribers" to the Exchange acting as the representatives or Agents of such Firms or Companies.

Rule C. If any Member of the Metal Exchange fails to meet his engagements to another Member, whether by failing to provide on the due date documents (*i.e.* Bills of Lading, Warrants or Delivery Orders according to the metals dealt in) to meet sales made or money to pay for metals bought, or by making default in fulfilling any other obligation arising out of dealings made subject to the Rules and Regulations of the London Metal Exchange, notice of the default shall be given at once in writing to the Committee of the Exchange and the Committee shall immediately fix and publish a settlement price or prices as at the date of such communication to them for all contracts which the defaulter may have open under these Rules, whether with Members or with parties who are not Members. All such contracts shall forthwith be closed and balanced, by selling to or buying from the defaulting Member such metals as he may have contracted to deliver or take, at the settlement prices fixed for this purpose by the Committee, and any difference arising whether from or to the party in default shall become payable forthwith notwithstanding that the prompt day or other day originally stipulated for the settlement of the transaction may not have arrived. In fixing settlement prices under this Rule the Committee may in their discretion take into consideration the extent and nature of the transactions which the defaulting Member has open and any other circumstance which they may consider should affect their decision. In any case where the Committee shall be of opinion that the default is not due to the insolvency of the defaulter the Committee shall by resolution negative the application of this rule. Any claim arising out of a default not due to insolvency shall be settled by arbitration in the usual manner. This rule shall apply to cases in which at or after the decease of a Member the engagements entered into by him are not duly met.

Rule D. In any Contract made subject to the Rules and Regulations of the London Metal Exchange between a Member and a non-Member in the event of the Mon-Member failing to meet his engagement arising out of any such contract whether by failing to provide on the due date documents to meet sales or money to take up documents (as the case may be) or otherwise howsoever or of his failing to supply or maintain such margin (if any) for which the Member is entitled to call and has called, or in the event of the Mon-Member's suspending payment or becoming bankrupt or committing any act of bankruptcy or (being a Company) in the event of its going into liquidation whether voluntary or otherwise, the Member shall have the right to close all or any such Contracts outstanding between them by selling out or buying in against the Non-Member (as the case may be) and any differences arising therefrom shall be payable forthwith notwithstanding that the prompt day or other day originally stipulated for settlement may not have arrived.

Rule E. Payments for Warrants or other documents (when deliverable under the Contracts) unless otherwise stipulated on the contract, shall be made by cash in London, or by cheque on a London *clearing* bank, either mode in Seller's option. The documents shall be tendered in London against the cash or cheque, as the case may be, and not later than 2.30 p.m. on the prompt or settling day.

Rule F. Contracts wherein Buyer or Seller (as the case may be) has the option to uplift or to deliver, prior to the prompt or settlement date by giving previous notice of his intention, shall have the notice reckoned by market days; such notices, unless otherwise stipulated at time of purchase or sale, shall be as follows: On a Contract with the option to uplift or to deliver during one calendar month or less, one day's notice shall be given; on a Contract with the option beyond one and up to two calendar months two days' notice shall be given; and on a Contract with the option beyond two and up to three calendar months three days' notice shall be given previous to the date on which delivery is required, or will be made. In the case of Silver on a Contract with the option beyond three and up to four calendar months four days' notice shall be given; on a Contract with the option beyond four and up to five calendar months five days' notice shall be given; on a Contract with the option beyond five and up to six calendar months six days' notice shall be given on a Contract with the option beyond six and up to seven calendar months seven days' notice shall be given previous to the date on which delivery is required, or will be made. Notice shall be given for the whole quantity stated in the contract and shall be tendered in writing and delivered at the office of the seller of the option not later than noon on the day of notice. Rent shall only be allowed to Buyer to actual day of settlement; and there shall not be any allowance of interest for a payment made prior to the prompt date.

Rule G. Prompt or settlement dates falling on Saturday, Sunday, or a

Bank Holiday, which days are not market days, shall be settled as follows. Prompts falling on Saturday shall be settled on the Friday previous; but should the preceding Friday be a Bank Holiday the prompt shall be extended to the Monday following; should both the Friday preceding and the Monday following be Bank Holidays, the prompt shall be settled on the Thursday previous. Prompts falling on Sunday should be extended to the Monday following, but should that Monday be a Bank Holiday the prompt shall be extended to the Tuesday following; should both the following Monday and Tuesday be Bank Holidays, the prompt shall then be extended to the Wednesday following. Prompts falling on a Bank Holiday shall be extended to the day following; and if the Bank Holiday fall on Friday the prompts shall be extended to the Monday following; but should the Friday be Good Friday, prompts falling on that day shall be settled on the Thursday previous. If Christmas Day falls on Monday, prompts falling on that day shall be extended to the Wednesday following, but if Christmas Day falls on Tuesday, Wednesday, Thursday, or Friday, prompts falling on that day shall be settled on the day previous.

Rule H. The establishment, or attempted establishment of a "corner", or participation directly or indirectly in either, being detrimental to the interests of the Exchange, the Committee shall, if in their opinion a "corner" has been or is in the course of being established, have power to investigate the matter and to take whatever action it considers proper to restore equilibrium between supply and demand. Any member or members may be required to give such information as is in his or their possession relative to the matter under investigation.

Rule J (OPTIONS). On the day on which notice is due, the holder of the option shall, except in cases to which Rule C applies, declare in writing before 12 o'clock noon whether he exercises or abandons the option, and if he fails to make such declaration the option shall be considered as abandoned. Options (subject to Rule F above) may be declared for less than the total optional quantity in quantities of 25 tonnes for Copper-Electrolytic Wirebars, HCFR Wirebars, Cathodes or Fire Refined, 5 tonnes for Standard Tin, High Grade Tin, 25 tonnes for Standard Lead, 25 tonnes for Standard Zinc and 10,000 ounces for Silver or multiples thereof, only one declaration against each contract being allowed. In cases to which Rule C applies the prices fixed by the Committee, at which outstanding contracts are to be closed, shall equally apply to all option contracts; and all options shall be automatically determined, and be deemed to have been either exercised or abandoned according as the prices may be in favour of or against the defaulter and whether the defaulter be the Seller or the Buyer of an option, and the option money shall be brought into account. In contracts with optional prompts, the price which shall be taken as the basis of settlement shall be the settlement price fixed by the

Committee under Rule C for the prompt most favourable to the holder of the option.

Rule K (CLEARING). All contracts made between Members of the London Metal Exchange who are entitled to deal in the Ring, either for Copper-Electrolytic Wirebars, HCFR Wirebars, Cathodes or Fire Refined, Standard Tin, High Grade Tin, Standard Lead, Standard Zinc or Silver, shall be settled through the Clearing, except when a Member insists on his right to receive cash instead of cheque from the Member to whom he has sold, in which case the Seller shall give notice to his Buyer before noon on the market day preceding the settling day, and such transactions shall then be exempted from settlement through the Clearing. The Rules governing the Clearing of all contracts shall be those in existence at the time fixed for the fulfilment of the contract. Copies of such rules may be obtained from the Secretary of the Exchange.

Rule L. In case of strikes, lock-outs, or other unforeseen contingencies in London, or other authorised port or point of delivery, which prevent or delay the discharge and/or warehousing of Copper-Electrolytic Wirebars, HCFR Wirebars, Cathodes or Fire Refined, Standard Tin, High Grade Tin, Standard Lead, Standard Zinc and/or Silver, the Seller may be allowed to postpone delivery if he can prove to the satisfaction of the Committee (of which proof the Committee shall be the sole judge) that he does not hold available metal in warehouse or vault with which to fulfil his contracts and that he has metal of the requisite quality which has arrived in London or any other authorised port or point of delivery at least ten days prior to the earliest prompt for which relief is asked, or has metal of the requisite quality in his works, but the delivery, discharge and/or warehousing of which is prevented or delayed as aforesaid. He must also deposit with the Secretary of the Exchange such sums as the Committee may require but not exceeding £5 per tonne in the case of Copper, Lead and Zinc, £10 per tonne in the case of Tin and £5 per thousand ounces in the case of Silver. No interest will be allowed on deposits, which will be returned after delivery of Warrants. Should his application be passed by the Committee, he shall deposit documents or other proof to the satisfaction of the Committee with the Secretary of the Exchange, who shall issue Certificates for Copper, Lead and Zinc in quantities of 25 tonnes, Certificates for Tin in quantities of 5 tonnes and Certificates for Silver in quantities of 10,000 ounces. The Seller shall deliver these Certificates to his Buyer. The Certificates will then constitute a good delivery on the Clearing within the period stated thereon and differences must be settled on the prompt day. The holder of a Certificate must present it to the firm named thereon not later than 2.30 p.m. on the day following that on which he receives notice in writing from his Seller that the Warrant for the actual Copper, Tin, Lead, Zinc or Silver is ready. He must take up the Warrant against payment at the settlement price fixed on the preceding market day, receiving or paying any difference between this and the price mentioned on the Certificate. In the event of the price on the Certificate being above or below the settlement price operative on the day of delivery the receiver shall pay or be paid the amount of any difference. No other payment shall pass except against delivery of the actual Warrant. In case of any dispute, the Committee's ruling to be final. A fee of £5 to be paid by the Applicants for each Certificate issued.

ARBITRATION

Rule 1. All disputes arising out of or in relation to contracts subject to the Rules and Regulations of the London Metal Exchange shall be referred to arbitration as hereinafter provided. The Executive Secretary of the Committee of the London Metal Exchange (hereinafter referred to as "the Secretary") shall be notified of such disputes in writing and the party first notifying the difference shall at the time of such notification deposit with the Metal Market & Exchange Co. Ltd., the sum of £100. All such disputes shall be referred to two arbitrators, one to be appointed by each party to the difference from the Arbitration Panel of the London Metal Exchange, such arbitrators having power to appoint a third arbitrator from the Panel and having all the powers conferred on arbitrators by the Arbitration Act 1950 or any statutory modifications thereof for the time being in force. The Secretary shall be notified in writing by each party of the appointment of the arbitrators. The arbitration and any Appeal made pursuant to Rule 8 of these Rules from the Award of the Arbitrators to the Committee shall take place at the London Metal Exchange (unless mutually agreed by the Arbitrators and the parties to the dispute that the venue should be elsewhere in England or Wales) and English procedure and law shall be applied thereto.

Rule 2. Persons eligible for appointment to the Arbitration Panel shall be members of the Exchange, their partners or co-directors (as the case may be) or members of their staff. Appointment to and removal from the Panel shall be made, at their sole discretion, by the Committee of the London Metal Exchange who will also be responsible for maintaining a panel of sufficient size.

Rule 3. In the event of either party to the difference (*a*) failing to appoint an arbitrator, or (*b*) failing to give notice in writing or by cable of such appointment to reach the other party within 14 days after receiving written or cabled notice from such other party of the appointment of an arbitrator (any notice by either party being given to the other either by cable or by registered post addressed to the usual place of business of such other party), or (*c*) in the case of death, refusal to act, or incapacity of an arbitrator, then, upon written or cabled request of either party an arbitrator shall be appointed from the said Arbitration Panel by the Committee of the London Metal Exchange.

Rule 4. In case the two arbitrators appointed as aforesaid, whether originally or by way of substitution, shall not within three calendar months

184

after the appointment of the arbitrator last appointed deliver their Award in writing, or choose a third arbitrator, then the said Committee on the written request of either party shall appoint a third arbitrator selected from the said Arbitration Panel to act with the two aforesaid arbitrators.

Rule 5. The Award in writing of the arbitrators or any two of them shall be made and delivered in triplicate to the Secretary within a period of three calendar months from the date of the acceptance of the appointment by the arbitrator last appointed.

Rule 6. Every Award made pursuant to any provision of this Rule shall be conclusive and binding on the parties to the arbitration, subject to appeal as hereinafter mentioned.

Rule 7. The procedure upon an arbitration shall be as follows:

(a) Within a period of 21 days after the appointment of the second of the two arbitrators so appointed, each party shall deliver to the arbitrators and to each other a statement of case in writing with the originals, or copies, of any documents referred to therein. All such documents to be in the English language or accompanied by certified translations into English.

(b) If either party shall make default in delivering such statements and documents (due consideration being given to time occupied by mails) the arbitrators shall proceed with the case on the statement before them, provided always that, in the sole discretion of the arbitrators, an extension of time may be allowed for the delivery of such statements and documents.

(c) The arbitrators shall appoint a day for a hearing within 28 days, or such further time as the arbitrators shall in their sole discretion allow, after the expiry of the 21 days in accordance with Rule 7(a), and shall give due notice in writing thereof to the parties, who may, and if required by the arbitrators shall, attend and shall submit to examination by the arbitrators and produce such books and documents as the arbitrators may require. Each party shall be entitled to produce verbal evidence before the arbitrators.

(d) Neither Counsel, nor Solicitor shall be briefed to appear for either party without the consent of the arbitrators.

(e) The arbitrators may engage legal or other assistance.

(f) The arbitrators may adjourn the hearing from time to time, giving due notice in writing to the parties of the resumed hearing, and the arbitrators may, if they think fit, proceed with such a resumed hearing in the absence of either party or of both parties.

(g) Where any change takes place in the constitution of the tribunal of arbitrators, either by substitution or otherwise, the new tribunal shall appoint a day for the hearing which shall be not later than 28 days, nor earlier than 7 days, after the change. Each party, if desiring to do so, may submit an Amended Statement of Case, with a copy to the other party, which must reach the new tribunal within seven days of its appointment.

(*h*) In the event of a third arbitrator being appointed, the provisions contained in Section 9 Sub-Section 1 of the Arbitration Act 1950 shall not apply to any reference.

(*i*) The cost of the arbitration shall be at the sole discretion of the arbitrators. The arbitrators shall fix the amount of their remuneration. The Award shall state separately the amount of such costs and remuneration and by whom they shall be paid and whether the whole or any part of the deposit referred to in Rule 1 of these Rules shall be returned to the party lodging the same or be forfeited. In the event of either or both parties having been granted permission by the arbitrators to be legally represented at the hearing the arbitrators may take into consideration any legal costs which have been incurred.

(*j*) The Award shall be deposited with the Secretary who shall forthwith give notice of receipt thereof in writing to both parties, and a copy of such Award shall be delivered to both parties on payment by either party of the costs specified in the Award, which payment shall not affect any provision of the Award.

(*k*) In the event that after the deposit referred to in Rule 1 of these Rules has been made the parties to the arbitration shall (i) settle their differences (ii) fail to proceed as directed by the arbitrators under sub-clause (*c*) of this Rule (iii) fail to take up the Award within 28 clear days of notification being given under sub-clause (*j*) of this Rule, such deposit shall be forfeited.

(*l*) At the time of issuing their Award, all statements and all documents lodged with the arbitrators shall be delivered by them to the Secretary, by whom they shall be retained until the expiration of the time for giving notice of appeal, as hereafter mentioned, after which the Secretary shall, unless there shall be such appeal, return them to the parties concerned.

Rule 8. Either party shall have the right to appeal against the Award to the Committee of the London Metal Exchange.

Rule 9. The method of appeal against the Award shall be as follows:

(*a*) The party making the appeal shall (*i*) within 21 days of the date of the Award give notice in writing of such appeal to the

Secretary, and to the other party and shall at the same time state the grounds for appeal. (*ii*) Deposit with the Secretary the sum of £200, and in addition the sum, if any, which shall be payable under the Award by the Appellant.

(*b*) Upon the receipt of such Notice of Appeal the Committee shall within 4 weeks nominate not less than five members, (hereinafter called "the Appeal Committee") to hear the Appeal. Members of the Appeal Committee shall be members of the Committee of the London Metal Exchange and/or members of the Board of the Metal Market & Exchange Co. Ltd.

(*c*) The procedure on appeal shall as far as possible be similar to that above provided for the original hearing, except that all statements and documents delivered to the Secretary under Rule 7 (*l*) shall be laid before the Appeal Committee, who may, however, require such further statement or statements or other information or documents from either or both of the parties as the Appeal Committee may think necessary. The provisions of Rule 7(*k*) shall apply in like manner to the deposit referred to in sub-paragraph (*a*) (ii) of this Rule as the deposit in connection with the original hearing.

(*d*) The decision in writing of the majority of the Appeal Committee (which latter shall not at any time number less than five) shall be final and binding on all parties, and the Appeal Committee shall also decide whether the whole or any part of the said deposit of £200 shall be returned to the Appellant or be forfeited.

(*e*) The Appeal Committee shall have the same discretion regarding costs as is given to the arbitrators under Rule 7(*i*) and shall fix the amount of their remuneration and direct by whom it shall be paid.

(*f*) All statements and all documents lodged with the Appeal Committee shall together with the Award, be deposited by them with the Secretary by whom they shall be retained until the costs and fees specified in the Award have been paid by either party. On payment, which shall not affect any provision of the Award, a copy of the Award shall be delivered to both parties and all documents returned to the parties concerned.

Index

Aluminium 153, 154
Amalgamated Copper Co. 38, 39
Anaconda 34, 39
Anglo-American Corporation 44
Anglo-Oriental Corporation 55
Arbitrage 95, 115, 151, 152
Arbitrations 16, 19, 30
Arrivals 29, 37, 99, 100
Asarco 74
Assay(ers) 19, 37
ASTM 37
Australia 70, 75, 76, 78
Australian tin 50, 51, 53
Authorised Clerk 16, 17, 21, 106

Back pricing (pricing terms) 104,
    136, 137
Backwardation 44, 57, 58, 119–
    126, 127–130, 135, 139
Baltic Exchange 9, 10
Bandoeng Pool 54, 55
Bank of England 60, 63, 84, 90,
    92, 93, 151, 152
Banka tin 51, 53
Belgium 42, 73, 74, 77, 79
Billiton tin 51
Board of Directors 11, 16–19, 82,
    94

Borrowing 120, 127–130
Brands 19, 29, 37, 54, 86, 107,
    120
British Metal Corporation 76
Bronze 7, 49
BSI 37
Budd, Sir Cecil 76

Canada 42, 44, 47, 76, 77, 78, 80,
    84
Carries 126, 127–130
Cartels 38–43, 55–60, 71–76, 77–
    80, 86
Cathodes (copper) 34–48
Chile 9, 34, 35, 37, 38, 42, 46, 47
Chile bar copper 29, 34–48, 100
China 56, 89
Chinese tin 53, 54
Class "A" tin 53
Class "B" tin 53
"Clearing", the 142, 143
Clearing house 18, 23–26, 104
CIPEC 47
Comex 89, 115
Committee of Subscribers 12, 13,
    15–18, 29, 52, 54, 79, 81, 82,
    90, 92–94, 106, 107, 151
Commodity shunting 83

Common tin   54
Contango   119–126, 127–130, 135, 139
Contracts   29–33, 52
Contract weights   141
Copper   7, 9, 11, 29, 34–48
Copper Exporters Inc.   40–42, 55
Corners   35, 36, 52
Cornish tin   50, 53

Delivery points   31, 37, 38, 86, 87, 100, 101, 107, 154, 155

EEC   47, 86, 149–151
Electro copper   38, 41, 42
Empire preference   78, 81, 82, 149
European Spelter Convention   73
Exchange control   151, 152
Executive Secretary of LME   16, 151
Executions   104, 111, 112, 127

Fabricator   32, 39, 124–126, 135, 136–139
Fire-refined copper   45
Force majeure   30
Foreign exchange   30, 92, 93, 95
France   36, 42, 73, 77

General Services Administration 65–67, 92
Gold Standard   78
Good merchantable brand (copper) 37, 38
Good merchantable quality (tin) 51, 53
Good ordinary brand (zinc)   86, 87
Good soft pig lead   72, 80, 86
Government (control, etc.)   13, 59–62, 74, 75, 82–84
Germany   40, 42, 44, 67, 70, 71, 73–79

Hedging   30–33, 100, 119–126

High conductivity fire-refined (copper)   45
High-grade (tin)   68

Imperial Smelting Co.   85
India   89
Indo-China   55
International Copper Cartel   43
International Tin Agreements   64–67, 68, 95
International Tin Committee   56–60
International Tin Restriction Scheme   56
International Zinc Cartel   78
Inter-Office Trading   104, 105

Japan   44, 82
Jerusalem Coffee House   9, 153

Kerb trading   103–104, 113–115
Korean War   61, 84

Lamb and flag tin   50
Lead   8, 11, 70–87
Lead Producers' Association   79
Lead Producers' Reporting Association   80
Lead Smelters' Association   74
Lead and Zinc Conference   85
Lead and Zinc Study Group   85
Lending   120, 127–130
Lombard Exchange and Newsroom 9, 10
London, City of   8, 9
London Silver Market (The Bullion Market)   11, 88-95, 107

Malay Straits   6
Malaysia   55
Membership of LME   16, 19–21, 156
Merton Brothers   71–76
Metal Market & Exchange Co. 12, 13, 14, 15

Metallgesellschaft 71, 74, 76
Mexico 70, 75, 79–80
Minor metals 103, 154
Minor Metals Traders' Association 154
Mixed tin 51, 52

Nickel 154
Nigeria 55

"Octopus", the 76
Options 161–166
Ottawa Conference 78, 79

Penang Tin Market ("The East") 63, 64
Peru 42, 47
Poland 77
Prices 10, 12, 112, 113
Pricing 32, 119–126, 167–171
Pricing terms (see Back-pricing)
Producers 123, 124, 137, 138

Quotations Committee 15, 16, 112

Refined copper 37, 38
Ring, the 11, 12
Ring trading 99–116
Royal Exchange 9
Rio Tinto Zinc Corporation 40
Rough copper 37, 38, 40
RST 44
Rules and Regulations of LME 16, 18–19
Russia (and Russian Bloc) 44, 47, 67, 150, 151

Second Tin Buffer Pool 59–60
Secondary copper 41–47
Secretan, Pierre 35–37, 53
Secretary of LME 10, 102, 112
Security of LME 22–26, 153
Settlement price (see also Pricing, Back-pricing and VAT) 119–126, 140–143, 144–149, 167–171

Silver 88–95
Silver Certificates 90
Smith, P. W. 84
Smith, P. G., CBE 84
Spain 39, 70–71, 72–74, 75, 79
Speculator (Speculation) 35–37, 101, 102
Spelter (see also Zinc) 11
Standard copper 34–48
Standard lead (contract) 86
Standard tin (contract) 53
Standing Committee 15
Stannaries, the 8, 50
Subscriptions to LME 10

Tariffs, etc. 78, 81–82, 149–151
Tin 7, 8, 9, 11, 49–69
Tin Buffer Pool 56, 58
Tin Buffer Stock Manager (see International Tin Agreements)
Tin Producers' Association 55, 56

United Nations (also UNCTAD) 47
USA 38–47, 55, 61–63, 70, 72, 73, 74, 75, 79, 80, 83, 84, 89, 90, 92

Value added tax 114–149
Virgin spelter contract 72, 86

Wirebars (copper) 34–48
Warehouses (also Warehouse warrants) 19, 31, 72, 100, 108, 150, 151, 154, 155
"White Contracts" 32, 33
Wolff, F. F., CBE 85
Wolff, J. D. 84
World War I 74–76
World War II 82

Zaire 44, 47
Zambia 44, 45, 46
Zinc (spelter) 11, 70–87, 100
Zinc Cartel 77